Not Enough Bullets

or

"We Kuykendalled 'um"

Hunting Tales from the Old Days in Texas,

from Buda to Cotulla to Marfa

and

Beyond

1925–1974

*Kit Carson Wallace—Hunting Camp, Colorado River
Bee Cave, Texas ca. 1890*

*Kit Carson Wallace—Bee Cave, Texas
ca. 1900*

Not Enough Bullets
Copyright © 2009 by Marshall E. Kuykendall

Marshall E. Kuykendall
900 Enchanted Oaks Dr.
Driftwood, TX 78619
Web Site: *www.CampfiresAndSippingWhiskey.com*
Facebook: *www.facebook.com/MarshallEKuykendall*

Cataloging-in-Publication Data

Kuykendall, Marshall E.—Not Enough Bullets

p.   cm.

Includes photographs and maps

I. Hunting—Texas. II. Texas—Hunting—Outdoorsmen
III. Texas—Ranches IV. Texas—Nature

ISBN 978-0-578-12315-8

SK 131 K66 2009   179.1K   LIC 2009912258

About the only two animals in the world you wouldn't want to 'Kuykendall' are the North American Grizzly and the Cape Buffalo of Africa.

—Dr. Raleigh R. Ross
Nairobi, Kenya, 1968

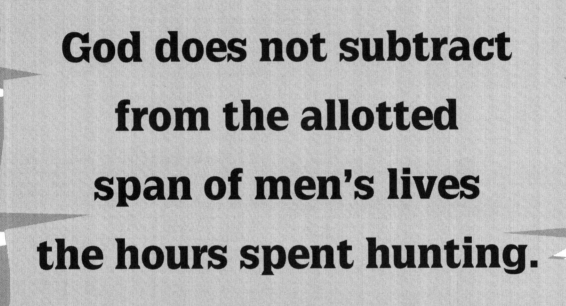

God does not subtract
from the allotted
span of men's lives
the hours spent hunting.

Contents

Dedication

This book is dedicated to my two best hunting companions in this lifetime, Jim Hairston and Bill Peace. They were with me throughout my early hunting days. I'm sure there was a time or two when they should have left me out on an ice-float for polar bear bait, but they didn't; and for that I am eternally grateful. Man, were they fine! They'd stay with you when everything went to hell in a handbasket and just laugh about it. Give Jim a beer and Bill some of his Meyers Rum and all was fine with the world. Both have gone to the "Happy Hunting Grounds" in the sky now. God, how I miss them! I will see them both down the dusty road a piece… But, not just yet!

A Brief Preface

These are hunting stories about a time in Texas when the ranches were big and rough and the men who hunted on them were the same. There were few roads and no deer stands. Wild game feeders and high fences did not exist, nor were there any exotic animals in Texas, other than a few Nilgai on the King Ranch. No one knew what a Jeep was until after World War II and no one ever he ard of a hunting lease. The deer were wild and few and far between. If you wanted to kill something, you got out in the brush and hunted all day on foot. You walked all day with nothing to eat and drank water out of the creek, if you found one. You sat on the damp ground or crawled up in the tree and hung your leg over a branch until the cramp got so bad you had to get down. When you got a chance to shoot at something you took the shot. If you didn't, the opportunity might not come your way again. When you killed something you field-dressed it and marked the spot so you or a ranch-hand could find it later. Some of the ways we hunted were unorthodox. I am not trying to glorify any of it nor take away any of the color. That's just the way it was back then.

This book is about a family who enjoyed hunting and the great outdoors tremendously. We thought there was nothing better in the whole world than getting out in the brush to see if we could outsmart ole' Mr. Buck. That was the same ole' Mr. Buck which outsmarted every predator and most men every day of his life because he did it for living. Normally, he won and we lost. That was the very nature of it, the challenge! And then, what is better than standing around a campfire later with old friends, sipping good whiskey and telling tall tales about how the "big one" got away. But do not think for one moment this is a "How to Do It" book; it is not! This is a *How We Did It* book.

Acknowledgements

About the time of the great War in 1941, Walter Glass somehow found out about my father and our Texas ranch and he decided to come down here from Albany, New York and take a bunch of pictures. He had the first 16mm movie camera I had ever seen and he spent quite some time with us taking reels of movie film all over our 11,000 acres. The ranch was still intact then and he found a willing participant in my father, who hauled him everywhere. In so doing, Dad also took Walter to Cotulla, Texas to meet Helen Storey and Sheriff Hogue Poole and join him in the fun of the times on a wild deer hunt or two. So, when Sarah Lee Storey Maltsberger of Cotulla called and told me she had

Not Enough Bullets

found a bunch of still photos and one reel of film Walter had taken in 1945 and, "Would I like to have a copy." I jumped at the chance.

When I received all of them, it occurred to me that I needed to sit down and write about a chapter in my life that was very important to me. I want to tell a story that only a few people know, and that was our early hunting life on the Kuykendall ranch and beyond. I am very obliged to my old friend, Sarah Lee, for lighting the spark that created this book.

My thanks to Pam Owens and the girls at Print Plus in Dripping Springs, Texas for organizing everything for me and getting my book to a point where it made sense.

I am also glad I was able to persuade Mike Cox of Austin, Texas to edit the manuscript for me. He ought to know how to do it after having written many fine books on Texas History and the Texas Rangers over the years. The only thing I couldn't figure out is why in the hell he wanted me to drop about half the cuss words in the book when they added such a nice flavor to it all. Damn!

And, I wish to thank my cousin, Cliff Logan of Austin, probably the best Southwestern art dealer known to mankind, for cajoling me over and over that this was something I needed to do.

To all: I am obliged!

The Other Story, Part I

I had to run like hell up the side of the arroyo. By the time I got to the top, I was out of breath with my tongue hanging out. The damn mule deer buck had peeked over the side and seen me. By the time I staggered out of there, he had crow-hopped out to about a hundred yards and was angling slightly to the left. He had quit bouncing and was by now in a smooth even pace with little puffs of volcanic dust blowing up from his feet. I unlimbered my ole' Winchester .270 as I slid to a stop, jerked up and snapped off a shot, trying not to "Kuykendall" him square in the butt. When I touched off the round, I was wobbling so bad I knew I'd shot underneath him. As I reached my left hand over the top to rack in another shell, the buck suddenly reared up on his hind legs, fell over backward, and jammed his horns in the ground as the dust kicked up all around him. I stood there with my mouth open trying to get my breath, wondering, *"What in the hell just happened?"* But, that is another story.

Not Enough Bullets

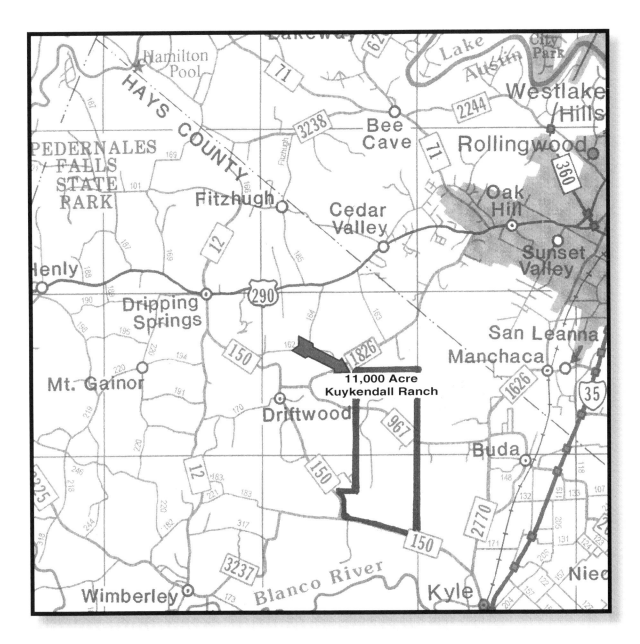

Kuykendall 101 Ranch

The Early Years

THE 101 RANCH
BUDA, TEXAS

Our ranch was just west of Buda and Kyle, Texas in Hays County. Grandfather Gil Kuykendall bought the 11,000 acres in 1901 after moving up from Matagorda County. When I arrived in the early 30's, times were hard and there was no money. When it came to providing food for the family, my father sure as hell wasn't going to kill a calf that might bring a dollar or three—not when we had a few deer, some wild hogs and strangely enough, some Spanish goats that were just as wild as the deer. I can not remember any time my father left the house that he didn't have his .30-30 with him. It was part and parcel of his every day get-up.

Every few days he would kill something, skin it out, cut it up and we had meat on the table. Alice (my mother) would cook up some rice or mashed potatoes, stew up a veggie or two and we would have venison back-straps with brown gravy. Makes me hungry just thinking about it.

One of the deer Dad killed in 1925 was pretty good sized. We had the horns nailed up in the horse barn as long as I can remember. He'd never paid any attention to any kind of records, but after several of his friends remarked that he ought to have the ole' buck scored for the record book, Dad whistled up one of his Texas game warden friends and asked him to do it. The buck had about a twenty-seven-inch spread and

Hays County Boone & Crockett Buck Killed by Bill Kuykendall in 1925 score: 176 5/8s

that was a pretty good deer by anyone's standards. A few days later the game warden called Dad and said, "Do you know that buck is good enough to enter the Boone and Crockett Club's records of North American Big Game?" Dad said, "No, what's that?" Well, sure 'nuff, the buck scored 176 and

Not Enough Bullets

101 Ranch, 1940
Pet Fawns—Bill Kuykendall

5/8s which made him good enough to be in the record book. In fact, to my knowledge it stands as the only Boone and Crockett buck ever killed in Hays County, Texas. (In the Boone and Crockett twelfth edition, Dad's deer is listed on page 424 under "Whitetail Deer-Typical Antlers.")

By the time I was six or seven, I could barely hold up a gun, so Dad got me a .25-20 caliber Winchester Model 92. Well, I was ecstatic. After he taught me how to hold and shoot it, I figured I was ready to use it.

Dad would catch a bunch of fawns every year, so we always had from one to a half-dozen that we fed on a bottle every day.

When Dad would milk, he'd fill some ole' brown beer bottles with fresh cow's milk and we'd all join in feeding the fawns. They'd stay around a while, but usually when they got to be yearlings, they'd wander off to be with their own kind. All of them but Darling.

Now Darling was the prettiest fawn you ever saw (hence the name) and as she approached her first year, she decided she liked us better than she did her own kin. So, as she matured over the next year or so, she'd wander off out into the pasture, but in the fall when the bucks went into rut and tried to squire little Miss Darling, she'd stick her tongue out at them and trot back up to the house and jump over the fence into our big yard. Well, she was so pretty that Mr. Buck would run right up to the yard fence and try and persuade Miss Darling to please come out and play.

One bright and cool morning when I was seven, Dad came and got me. I saw he was carrying my trusty little carbine. He told me to be real quiet, that Miss Darling had one of her suitors with her and we were going to nail him. Dad cracked open the front door of our house, which looked out and down over our 1,200-acre front pasture. Sure enough, right over the fence stood Mr. Bucky, all bright-eyed and bushy tailed. Dad levered in a shell for me, cracked the front door about an inch, and said, "There he is, Son, shoot him." I stuck that little gun through the crack, closed both eyes I'm sure and touched one off. God and the Indian Spirits were kind to me that day because I hit him just above his heart and killed that sucker dead as a hammer. Dad howled in delight and my hunting days were off and running, big time.

The Early Years

MEK — 1st Buck
101 Ranch 1942

Gun Etiquette

Gun manners are just like any other manners and they were taught to me early and often. Our guns were always loaded and we treated them as such.

When I was growing up, there were always guns in our ranch house but I never touched them. That is not something that the current culture can tolerate. These days guns in the house around children need to be unloaded. However, the concept of having a house gun for protection that is locked away in one place with the bullets locked up somewhere else is ludicrous. You might as well go down by the creek and pick up a pretty round rock about the size of a softball and have it beside your bed at night in case you need it.

Dad was a stickler for gun safety. He was a great hunter, knew what guns were for and knew how dangerous they could be if handled improperly.

What he told me was this, and I'll pass it along: NEVER point ANY gun at ANYONE! When I was a boy, there was no sit-down hunter safety school for youngsters to attend. But, I was in school every day of my early life with my father, who was very strict about gun safety. His comment a thousand times, was "one mistake is ONE mistake too many and IT will kill you or

Not Enough Bullets

101 Ranch deer—1938
Gardner Abbott & Bill Kuykendall

someone else." Real simple. "Don't point ANY gun at ANYONE," Dad would say, "or, ONE, I will take your gun away from you, and TWO, whip the hell out of you."

I figured that was enough safety incentive to last a lifetime.

Dad also taught me that the handling of rifles and shotguns is different from the handling of pistols. That is something very difficult to learn. It comes only from years

and years of practice and understanding how much fun it is to hunt and shoot.

The problem with pistols is you can swing the barrel so easily with your body, so as you turn to face someone with a pistol in your hand, the tendency is to swing the gun in that direction. Dad taught me to dip the barrel down as I turned. Takes years or a long time to where it becomes natural. I still possess that habit. If I have a pistol in my hand, you can holler at me, I will jump and turn but that barrel will automatically swing down.

Rifles are different because of their size and the length of the barrels. One has a tendency to be more careful, however, an example: We never carried our rifles barrel up in the truck or jeep. Folks will tell you, "Oh, don't put the barrel down on the floor, you will get mud in the barrel." So they ride along in the truck or jeep, with the rifle butt on the floor between their knees and the end of the barrel, floating right under their chin. As Dad said, "Better to blow the mud out of the barrel than to blow your damn head off." We always put our barrels down on the floor.

Getting out of a truck, most folks will ease out and drag their rifle or shotgun behind them, which causes the barrel to stay in the truck—sometimes pointed back at the driver. We always swung the rifle barrel out first. The ole' man knew what he was doing when it came to guns. And thanks to him, I do too.

Friends

All of Dad and Alice's social lives revolved around Austin. If any friend ever showed up to hunt that person would be from there. Dad was a good neighbor but he wasn't one to ever go into Buda and sit around the pot-bellied stove at the feed store and spit tobacco juice into a Maxwell House coffee can. Just wasn't his style.

*Bill Kuykendall
M-64 Winchester Rifle*

One of the first people I remember who was out hunting with Dad all the time was Sis Robinson. Sis was a member of the Robinson clan, who own Austin White Lime. Her real name was Flora, but I never knew it until I was grown because she was always just "Sis." She and her mother, Mama Al, (Mrs. Alfred) lived in one of the old, beautiful three-story antebellum homes on the southwest corner of the Bremond block of West 7th Street in Austin. I have spent many a day there. Alice would drop me off there if she had to go shopping and pick me up when she was ready to go back to the ranch. I have very fond memories of that wonderful old house and those two fine women.

One day I'm in the house reading about the

Not Enough Bullets

Royal Canadian Mounties or Jack O'Brien's classic Spike of Swift River when Dad and Sis came busting in the house to get me. Seems Dad and Sis had just driven up from making a hunting tour and as they parked the pickup, Dad looked out over the corrals toward the front pasture and there was a hell of a good buck drinking out of the horse-trough. Dad wanted Sis to kill him, but bless her soul, she said, "No, let's go get Marshall."

Dad had my .25-20 in his hand and the two of them drug me out beyond the garage and wash shed toward the pens where we could get a peek at that ole' buck. Sure enough he was still there. Dad had me get down and he stuck the barrel of my little pea-shooter through the rails of the fence. I aimed at the buck, closed both eyes, squeezed off a shot and hit him just behind the shoulders. He turned out to be the biggest buck I ever killed on the Hays County ranch. He had ten points and about a twenty-inch spread. I was ten years old and would not have had that opportunity had it not been for Sis Robinson.

Ranchers Versus Hunters

There are ranchers who are ranchers, ranchers who are cowboys and a few ranchers who are hunters. I was surprised growing up to run into so many ranchers who just couldn't stand people who hunted. Well, I'm here to tell you that wasn't the way it was with the Kuykendall clan. We ranched like hell till September 1st, and then sat out on the old tank dam hoping a pin-feathered dove would fly in from the north-pole so we could get a whack at him. I have sat around that damn tank when it was 103 in the shade, with sweat running down my back, just daring anything to fly by.

In those days, mourning dove season started in the North Zone on September 1, and deer season started on November 16; it didn't matter what day of the week it was. Then, white-tailed deer season lasted until sundown on December 31. Thrown in between, in deep West Texas, was the desert mule deer season, which lasted only three or four days, usually around Thanksgiving weekend.

So, our "Physical" year started with hoops and hollers on September 1 and ended with much squalling and gnashing of teeth on December 31. During the middle time, you'd better not stand in the way.

Bill Kuykendall — 101 Ranch, 1938

8

The Early Years

An Early Lesson

By the time World War Two had started, I was old enough to wander off into the pasture by myself, still packing the .25-20. There are certain lessons you learn early on and one of the most important ones is to never and I mean NEVER, get separated from your gun. I don't care what you are doing when you are in the woods, always keep your rifle within arms length. You never know what you are going to see or what's gonna see you. In other words, when you need that rifle, you're really going to need it.

The Call of Nature

A funny case in point has happened to me more than once and I am sure it has happened to every hunter who's ever gone into the woods. You are all bundled against the cold and just getting into some of the best part of your hunting country when you hear this melodious sound come floating down through the woods from, you guessed it, the Call of Nature. There is a sudden pang in your gut and you realize you got to take that call, OR ELSE!

So, what do you do? Well, you ease around looking for the right spot that kinda has you hidden. You take off about thirteen layers of clothing, being careful to lay your coat over the nearest bush so it won't touch the ground and get wet. Then you lean you rifle either over against your coat, barrel up, or in a little v-notch in another bush nearby, being careful, again, not to lay it flat on the ground, cause it will get damp and get dirt on the side of it. Then you start undoing your belt and un-zipping your pants, all the while looking around for a clear place to squat so no grass stalks will tickle your butt. You get all situated and have now squatted down to do your business. You have spread out your feet as wide as the pants down around your ankles will allow. You then commence to try and get through this ordeal, all the while shaking and trembling like an old hog trying to pass a peach seed.

About that time you hear a little tiny noise and look up. There, standing about eight feet in front of you is a very nice buck with his hair all standing up ready to fight. He has either heard you break off some bushes or has come to protect his territory. What you didn't realize was with all your preparation, you have moved about seven feet from your rifle—well beyond arm's length. Damn! Your pants are hanging around your ankles. You take a quick look at Mr. Buck who is still trying to figure out whether to charge you or run. You sneak a peek at your gun which is out of reach and ease up trying not to fall or step in your own creation. You try to waddle over to get your hand on your rifle when Mr. Buck decides this is just too crazy and snorts a snort that will run everything out of the pasture, whirls and runs away. So, there you are, still squatting, pants now down on the ground, with just the gun barrel in your hand. The buck that was an easy kill is gone and you have messed up big time in more ways than one.

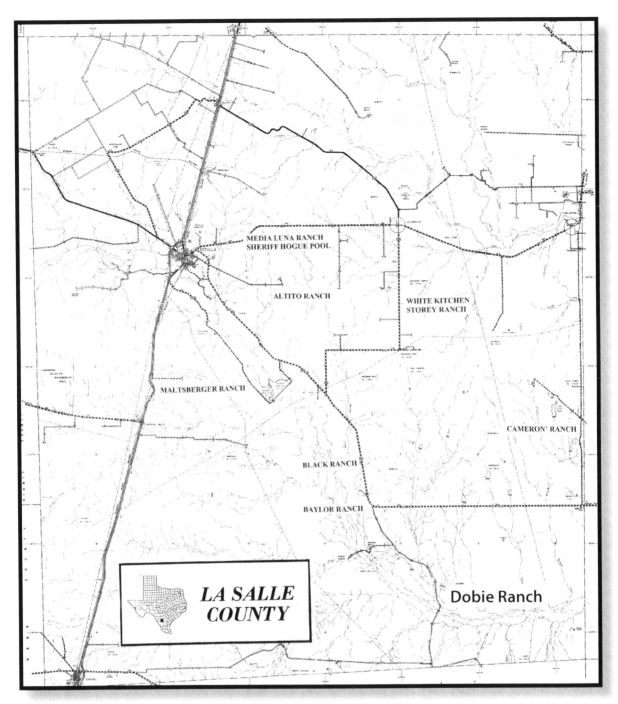

Dobie Ranch Map—1945

The Early South Texas Years

THE DOBIE RANCH

One of the greatest times I had in my early years was during the latter part of the Great War (1945) when Dad would go down to Cotulla to hunt with Hogue Poole and Helen Storey. I think Uncle Hogue, as I called him, was still the High Sheriff of La Salle County, and I'm here to tell you he was a booger. Helen Storey was a pretty interesting person in her own right. One of Dad's best buddies was LaVerne Allen of Kyle. LaVerne was married to Helen's aunt, so friends and families were mixed all together.

Anyway, in about 1945, Hogue and Helen had gotten the right to hunt on the 50,000-acre Dobie Ranch just southeast of Cotulla. Dad and LaVerne got invited down to join in the festivities.

Now, you might wonder, how a thirteen-year-old kid gets to go with all these grown-ups. Well, it's simple. One, they couldn't leave me at the Buda ranch by myself, and two, I stammered. I don't think I uttered a complete sentence until I was fifteen... If you had been raised by my father you would have stammered too, but that is another story.

For those of you who don't have a clue about the difference between one who stutters and one who stammers, I will simplify it for you. A stutterer makes noises and the words are garbled when they come

Dobie Ranch sign

out, but a stammerer opens his or her mouth to say something and nothing comes out. In my case, it's called Kuykendall Vapor Lock. Happens all the time, open up to say something, and *voilà,* nothing! Well, if you were my father, who really didn't have a lot of patience with man or beast, having a little snotty-nosed kid around was bad, but the kid could be tolerated if the little devil just didn't ever talk or make any noise. Also, I don't know about you and your family, but in mine if you could talk, it was limited to "Yes, Sir, No, Sir, Yes, Ma'am, No, Ma'am" or you got your butt whipped right quick. So, either you never said anything or you said the above. All of this is a long way of explaining one of the reasons I was allowed on the hunt. Besides Uncle Hogue would get

Not Enough Bullets

all sauced up on some really good whiskey and holler, "Marshall, go fight them damn flies." Turns out he had seen me out where all the deer were hanging one day, trying to bat the flies away and it stuck with him. So, he invited Dad to hunt on the Dobie Ranch, and said, "By the way, bring your son down here so he can fight them damn flies." See, kids are good for something.

Helen Storey & Sheriff Hogue Pool

Hunting Car—Dobie Ranch 1945
Kassie Keithley, Alice Kuykendall
Helen Storey, Hogue Pool

Uncle Hogue would ease out into one of the big pastures and we'd commence to poke along in his converted convertible until we jumped something. As luck would have it, on one of the days I was allowed to ride we drove up on a bunch of does. Trailing along with them was a hell of a big buck. With no hesitation whatsoever, Uncle Hogue threw that little Mercury into Hurry-up and the race was on.

Fair Chase, South Texas Style

For those who think you know how to hunt, let me help you out a tad. You ain't seen nothing 'til you got in Uncle Hogue's '41 Mercury convertible. It had a steel pan all the way underneath it with all four tires filled with some gunk used in military Jeeps to keep them from going flat. He'd load Helen in the front and me and Dad in the back. Helen always shot a little short 6.5 mm Austrian Mannlicher-Schoenauer with a flat bolt and the wood extending out to the end of the barrel. Dad was still shooting his Model 64 .30-30.

Dobie Ranch 1945
Sheriff Hogue Pool and MEK

12

The Early South Texas Years

Dobie Ranch 1945
Alice Kuykendall, Bill Kuykendall, MEK

Dobie Ranch Hunting Camp 1945
Walter Glass, Alice Kuykendall, Captain Marsh (with dog), Unknown
Sheriff Hogue Pool, Helen Storey, Roy Martin, Kassie Keithley, MEK, Bill Kuykendall

Not Enough Bullets

Boone & Crockett Trophies—1945
Dobie Ranch

Dobie Ranch Hunters—1945
LaVern Allen, Helen Storey, Bill Kuykendall, Sheriff Hogue Pool
In front of Old Ice House, Cotulla, Texas

The Early South Texas Years

He whirled that sucker out into the black-brush and in about fifty yards we were practically tapping that ole' buck in the butt with the front bumper with Uncle Hogue hollering at the top of his lungs to Helen, "SHOOT, DAMMIT, SHOOT!" We must have run that deer for a half-mile when we came to a big draw. With no hesitation at all, Uncle Hogue swerved around the head of it. Finally we caught sight of Mr. Buck about two hundred yards ahead. Uncle Hogue poured the coals to the little Mercury and ran through the biggest pear flat I have ever seen. If you had looked back, you would have seen a big hole cut through the pear just the shape of the car, windshield and all. Then the buck made a big all-out turn to the right with us turning with him. As we rolled out straight, Uncle Hogue again let 'er fly. Just then Helen stood up and took another whack at him over the windshield and damn if she didn't shoot off about half of his right horn. That caused the deer to go ass-over-tea-kettle in a big cloud of dust. Uncle Hogue then drove that little Mercury right up on top of him. Helen piled out and put another bullet into him and the damnedest run you have ever witnessed in the South Texas brush country was over.

That was what you would call wild and woolly hunting. If you think I'd ever forget that experience as a thirteen-year-old, you are sadly mistaken. As I said, Uncle Hogue was a booger, no doubt about it. It was what it was, wild men, wild deer and wild times. I'm not trying to judge it, just simply telling the story, as I remember it.

Not Enough Bullets

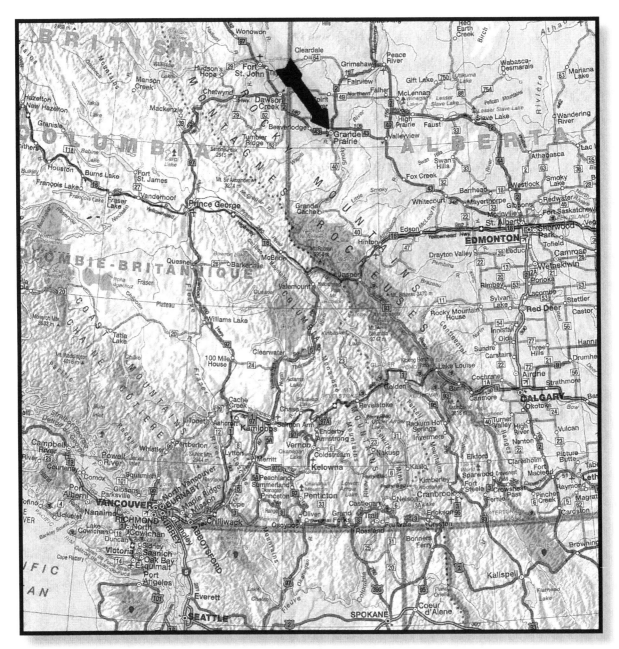

Bill Kuykendall's
Canada Hunt — 1948

Dad's Canadian Hunt

Dad got an opportunity to on a grand horseback hunt in Alberta, Canada in 1948. He whistled up two of his doctor friends from Austin, Dr. Bob Morrison and Dr. Paul Robison and the three of them drove north to Canada.

Before he left, Dad had to upgrade his weaponry. He knew his trusty .30-30 wouldn't be the right gun for this hunt. One day, while Dad and neighbor Cecil Ruby were visiting, Mr. Ruby mentioned he had just the right gun for Dad to take. It was a pre-war Super Grade Model 70 Winchester in .270 caliber, one of the flattest-shooting guns ever produced by Winchester. Dad was thrilled.

So off he and his friends went for a forty-five-day sojourn into the outback of that part of Canada. In those days, there were no roads into the northwest area of Alberta or northeast British Columbia. Dad and his bunch drove all the way through Edmonton and on northeast to Grande Prairie, Alberta where Kelly Sunderman lived. Sunderman had been a professional outfitter for many years and had a fine reputation.

The hunt was like something out of a Charles Russell drawing: Hunters on horseback up in the Rockies with the pack-train pulling up the rear, fully packed with everything folks would need for a month long hunt. I think Dad told me besides the three of them, there were Sunderman, five or six

Canada Hunt
Bill Kuykendall—1948

helpers and a string of forty-five horses—riding stock and pack animals. Dad said it was fantastic.

I think they rode out from Grande Prairie. Dad said the trip into the wilderness hunting area took several days. Each evening, when they got to a good camping spot, the cook got off his horse first and the others followed. The first pack horses they unloaded were for the cook: tent, stove, food,

Not Enough Bullets

Canada Hunt
Dr. Bob Morrison 1948

and other items he needed. While the rest of the pack string was being unloaded, the cook would be rustling up supper. That was the procedure each day until they finally reached good hunting country. Then a more permanent camp was set up.

The hunt was for mountain sheep, mountain goat, moose and bear. The first few days out, Sunderman told Dad he wanted him to kill a mule deer for camp meat. So the two of them wandered not far out of camp where they spotted several young bucks running together. Dad took aim with his .270 with open sights and fired. Sunderman, said,

"You missed him, shoot again." Not to argue with the man, Dad fired again. They walked up the side of the mountain a short distance and there lying in the tall grass were two very dead, very fat young bucks. Sunderman said, "Damn! Well, I told you to shoot again and shoot you did." He and Dad became very good friends from that point on. The old man now knew my dad could shoot, so for the rest of the hunt, Dad was the designated "meat-getter." Sundermann was so taken by this crazy Texan that he invited Dad to return for a second hunt in 1949 at no charge just so Dad could ride with him into the outback.

Back at the 101

FROM OPEN SIGHTS TO SCOPES

As I got older and bigger, so did my gun. Dad sold the 3,600-acre home pasture to Pat Rutherford of Houston in 1948 and we moved to the south side of the ranch. By that time, I had migrated from the Model 92 Winchester .25-20 to a fine .250-3000 Savage. And man, it was hot. While the .25-20 is a neat little cartridge, it is really only good for short distances and too light to really bring down a big buck. But, I'm here to tell you that .250-3000 will put the hurt on an old buck and make him hump-up pretty good. So, I was popping as many as I could.

In those days, you could only take antlered animals and the buck had to have at least three points. It was against the law to kill a doe or a spike (a two-pointer.) What made that interesting was that you had to stop and think when you got that hurried glimpse at a deer. So type recognition was imperative. Sure made everyone a better hunter.

Back in the 1940s none of our rifles had scopes on them. The idea of having a scope was foreign to us. Heck, we couldn't see through one of them if we had had one. Dad had killed everything he could in Canada with open sights. When he got home, for some reason, he switched to a Remington .30-06 and gave me the Winchester .270 he had gotten from our neighbor. I think Dad wanted a little heavier bullet, which the .30-06 offered.

Dad's sister, Dorothy K. Hoskins, lived over in another part of the ranch with Dad's mother, Maggie Kuykendall. Also living there with them was my crazy cousin Worth Hoskins, Dorothy's son. Worth had been in the Army during the war, but did not serve anywhere that could have gotten him killed. Worth could build or fix anything. He could build a car, a bulldozer, or a rifle. He had a little shop in the backyard toward the milking pens where he had a lathe and all the fixings. About the time Dad got home from Canada, Worth was into building guns of all types and he had acquired a bunch of scopes for different rifles.

I was over there one day and Worth told me he'd give me a scope for my .270 if I'd let him put it on for me. I said, sure! So, he installed my first scope, which was a Lyman/Alaskan 2.5 power with a Lee Dot. What that meant was my scope was very low powered, and meant it was easy to learn to see and shoot through. The Lee Dot was a little round black dot in the center of the cross hairs in the scope. All you had to do was sight the gun, look through the scope and when you saw the animal or target, put the Lee Dot where you wanted to shoot, and pull the trigger. Sounds easy, "don't it?"

I practiced until I got where I could finally see a moving deer through the scope but it took a while. Now, it's as easy as pulling the gun up to your shoulder and the deer is already in the picture. We all wonder now how anyone ever shot with open sights.

In the 1920s, '30s, and '40s, if it slithered, slid, crawled, hopped, jumped, ran or flew, we shot at it. If it was good to eat, we ate it; if it wasn't, we shot at it anyway. Just the way it was. Dad especially hated armadillos because one of his horses had stepped in an armadillo's hole one time and broke its leg. So, as Will Rogers surely would have said, "I have never met an armadillo I didn't want to shoot at."

About the time I was old enough to get involved, Cousin Worth was into souping up his rifles. If it shot at 2,800 feet per second like my .270 did, he wanted it shooting 4,000 feet per second. So he was hand loading all his own bullets. Unfortunately, they got so hot (fast), they'd break up coming out of the barrel. We were riding around his place one day and we spotted an armadillo. He said, "Watch this." Then he poked his souped-up .30-06 out the window, put the cross hair on Mr. Armadillo, and touched 'er off. When that .30-06 bullet hit that armadillo traveling at about nine zillion feet per second there was nothing but pink vapor left. No armadillo, no nothing. Worth had to slack off on the speed cause the next day he shot a buck with it and the bullet was so hot it exploded on the outside of his skin, doing nothing but blowing the hair off. I'm not trying to dramatize it here, just telling a story.

The Way We Hunted Back Then

Deer leases had not been invented yet. I never sat in a so called deer stand. Dad might have a board nailed up in a tree someplace, but I don't remember. And no one saw a Jeep until after the Great War. We didn't even know what four-wheel drive was.

We hunted either out of the pickup or we walked. Dad would drive around until we spotted some deer and he'd slow down until we passed a cedar bush or something and have me slip out behind that bush while he was still moving. That way, the buck would look at the pickup and not at me and I might get a shot.

We did this all the time, but my favorite way to hunt was always on foot. I hunted every single day of the season. As soon as I got off the school bus or got through with football practice, or whatever it was I was doing, I went hunting.

Bullets

Most rifles hold six cartridges when fully loaded, five in the magazine and one in the chamber. We all wore blue jeans or Levi's in those day and all Levis had a little watch pocket sewed in above the right hand pocket. If you put extra shells in your pocket, they would rattle when you walked and were hard to get out. But the little watch-pocket was perfect, because it would hold four or five rounds... There they wouldn't make any noise and were easily extracted. Only a few people had the leather or canvas cartridge holders you see today that attach to your belt.

Since I was a "hot-shot" hunter, I would laugh when Dad's friends would show up all dolled up in their hunting duds and sporting a new leather cartridge holder that held an additional twenty rounds. *Man*, I thought, *that's 25 or 26 total bullets. If those crazies can't hit them with that many, we're in big trouble.*

Since game identification was important here in Texas, meaning you could not take a doe or spike, indiscriminant shooting was rare. Those of us who have hunted most of our lives have heard tales of folks who venture into the brush completely out of their element. They will shoot at anything, anybody or any sound they hear. I had never encountered it. Well, that was about to change.

"Sound Hunting"

Dad was friends with a very prominent judge in the area. After we were settled in our new home on the south side of the ranch, Dad invited the good judge and his son out for a hunt. The judge had done Dad a favor I am sure and Dad was trying to repay him for his kindness.

It fell to me to haul them over to our west pasture—we called that part of the ranch the Nook—and pick them up after dark that same day. The bunch showed up at our house before daylight, but we had the coffee ready. After a brief visit around the kitchen table, I loaded the judge and his son into our Jeep and drove them over to the Nook pasture. We were in the process of clearing the cedar in that pasture but there was still a bunch of it there, so it was pretty brushy. Standing in the middle of the pasture was the windmill, which I thought would be a good place for them to start hunting. I dumped them out, wished them well, told them I'd pick them up just after sun-down, and off I went.

It must have been a Saturday, because I went hunting in the adjacent pasture called the Potter Spring pasture. After it got good and light, I piddled around down by the spring where I had seen a good buck. I noted several shots coming from over in the Nook pasture and thought our guests must be having a good day. Nothing was coming my way, so I went home for lunch.

About three o'clock that afternoon I went back to the Potter and soon heard one or two more shots. I figured they must have cornered something fierce over there, but I really paid it no mind. The sun started to set and when it got just dark enough for me to turn on the headlights, I went back into the Nook pasture. I had opened the gate on FM 150 and was making my way to the windmill, lights on bright, so they'd see me, and just as I approached the mill, BAM-BAM went off right in front of me and I saw the flash of the guns as they fired. By that time it was pitch-black dark. I was only a teenager but it did get my dander up a bit. As I shined the lights on the pair, I could see them aiming again off to one side, so I flashed the lights, pulled up to the judge, and said rather angrily, "Judge, Sir, what in the world were you and your son shooting at?" Both had big grins on their faces and spoke almost together, "We heard a noise over there as you were driving up!" I was shocked. I then asked them how many deer they had killed that day and they said, "None," but they had gotten some really great "sound shots" that day and sure had a ton of fun. Remembering that we had two horses over there rummaging around I asked if by chance they had seen or shot at the horses, and with an excited look on his face, the Judge said, "I don't think so!"

So, I'm here to tell you friends, there are some crazies out there. Maybe that's why some of the old ranchers don't like hunters. When I got back to the house I reported to Dad what had transpired and those folks were never invited back on the Kuykendall ranch again.

Game Conservation in Texas

No state in the lower forty-eight is more concerned with game conservation than Texas. Since Texas is a private property state, it falls to the landowners to assist the state in managing its diverse wildlife populations, which by and large are the best in the nation. In current times, Texas has, in addition to the native game, one of the largest exotic populations of African and Indian animals in the world outside of those two foreign countries. This was not always the case.

Before and spilling over until just after World War II, there was a tremendous amount of hunting all year long, without regard to state-set seasons or regulations. In a hold over from earlier days, old timers still ran a few dogs after deer and some outlaws figured they could hunt anywhere and anytime they damn well pleased.

Well, that was about to change. Dad had decided by the late 1930s that the Kuykendall 11,000 acres was off limits to uninvited hunters. It was private property and it was his feeling that folks ought to ask permission to come on his or his sibling's part of the ranch. By the time we moved to the south side of the ranch in 1947, he had had a run in or two with some of the outlaw types and folks who wanted to hunt whenever and wherever. They suddenly had an adversary in my father.

One early case in point: Just before we moved to the south side, Dad and a ranch-hand saddled up one night and rode over south of Onion Creek because Dad had gotten word some fellows were going to sneak in over there. Dad always carried his .30-30 and sometimes carried a .32-20 single-action Colt revolver. That night he lent his six-shooter to the ranch-hand. They eased over to what we called the Lock Pasture, stepped off their horses, tied them and commenced to slip up on two old boys who were head-lighting. Dad had seen their lights as they flashed down through the trees. He and old One Ear (the ranch-hand had his left ear missing) got down in front of the fellows and waited. As luck would have it, the trespassers angled into One Ear. When he rolled over a bit to get a better look at them, the outlaws heard a branch snap and fired off a shot at the sound. The bullet went through his jacket burning a big gouge across his upper arm. At the same instant, ole' One Ear let fly with Dad's trusty six-shooter and shot the flashlight out of the outlaw's hand. Then a big run-off occurred and the fellows got away.

The next day, Dad drove into San Marcos and whistled up the High Sheriff and they went looking for the fellows they thought had been on the ranch. When they located them, the main ruffian had his right forefinger bandaged up. Told the Sheriff he had cut it on a Coke bottle.

Part of the problem in those years was that when trespassers got caught, the offense was a misdemeanor and the fine amounted to only a few dollars. So, Dad got together with a bunch of local ranch owners, one of whom was Charles Morton, who lived over near Cedar Valley, and they formed what was known as the Hays-Travis County Game Protective Association.

They then persuaded the county judges in both counties to raise the trespass fine from something like $25 to $250. When word began to spread that hunting out of season and trespassing was going to get a bit more expensive in Central Texas, a howl went up from the "I'm gonna hunt anytime I damn well please" folks.

Dad and the group hired a gunfighter from Llano County by the name of Dean Smith as "Special Warden" for the association. I think Dean had been a Texas Ranger at one time. He and Dad had been buddies for years. That quiet little man was one tough son of a bitch and I mean that in the most endearing terms. I was in awe of him and so were the potential law breakers. You didn't mess with Dean Smith. He'd jerk your damn ears off and make you eat them and then he'd stick his six-shooter in your mouth and whisper to you he didn't think you ought to trespass on so and so's ranch anymore. Kinda took all the fun out of it; along with the new high-dollar fine.

Then the inevitable happened. Just after we had moved to the south side of the ranch, I got up one morning to get ready for school and the whole back yard of our ranch-house was full of sheriff's cars. Mother told me to stay in the house because there had been some trouble over in the Nook Pasture.

Seems that Dad had gotten word that some outlaws were going to come in that previous night and head-light in the Nook

pasture. I asked Dad how he had known about these folks and all he said was, "They left signs like deer guts in our mailbox or a cedar branch hung in the fence over on the west side." Anyway, I never did get a definitive answer on how he knew these fellows were gonna be there that night but he knew. He knew so well, in fact, that he had called the Texas Rangers a few days before and was on record as having asked for their assistance. They were unable to oblige.

Turns out, when Dad heard he was going to have some uninvited visitors and no one else would come to his aid, he called his brother Ike, who now lived over near Dripping Springs and his nephew, my cousin Worth. They had all gone over into the Nook pasture the night before and were waiting for the outlaws to show up and show up they did. The only minor problem was they showed up in front of Dad.

The official version, as I understood it, was that two fellows from the metropolis of Driftwood, both known as pretty good outlaws, had slipped over into the Nook pasture. The fellow in front had killed a small deer and was carrying it over his shoulder with his gun in his off hand. He either had a flashlight or a head-light, I don't remember which.

The Shooting

Well, he walked right up to Dad and when he did Dad shined a powerful flashlight in his face and told him to stop. Knowing Dad, he probably said, "I got you, you sonofabitch." The instant that happened, the fellow unraveled the deer from his shoulder and jerked up his rifle to shoot. But Dad let fly with his .30-30 and blew him into the next county. I'm here to tell you that being shot in the gizzard with a 180-grain, soft-point bullet traveling

Game Conservation in Texas

at 1,800 feet per second will break a man of a bunch of bad habits. That fellow's days as a trespasser were over.

In the run-off that occurred immediately thereafter, the second man boogered so badly that he was not found until the next day. When he finally surfaced, most of his clothes had been ripped off from running wildly through the lovely cedar breaks of the Texas Hill Country. I guess that's better than a .30-30 bullet up your butt. The poor fellow probably went home and hid in his root cellar for a month.

A few days after the incident my father was relating what had happened to his good friend, Captain Frank Hamer, late of the Texas Rangers and Captain Frank said, "Bill, how come you didn't shoot that other feller?" Dad said, "Well, he was running off, Cap." Hamer then slightly admonished my father and said, "Bill, outlaws are outlaws, and they are just as dead shot from the back as they are shot from the front." That old man ought to have known—he'd been in about a hundred gun fights in his life.

Needless to say, that little incident, along with the new high-dollar trespassing fine,

put a real damper on the practice of "hunting when and where you damn well pleased." The outlaw groups had finally gotten the message that the price of hunting illegally in Texas was getting a tad higher than they could afford.

After that, more and more ranch owners got involved in protecting the game they had and the population of white-tailed deer greatly expanded into what is one of the better populations in the country today. A lot of it was because my Dad and Charles Morton took offense at folks who thought they could come on your property any time they damn well pleased and get away with it unscathed.

Very few present Texas ranch owners know that the reason they can enjoy the game they have today and the laws they have that protect them came largely from those two men, along with that the little gunfighter from Llano County, Dean Smith. He was one tough, little dynamite stick and the fuse was always lit.

A Hays County grand jury was empanelled and Dad was no-billed for killing the trespasser who had pointed a rifle at him.

Not Enough Bullets

*Texas Ranger Frank Hamer, photographed the day after
he killed Ed Putnam at Del Rio.
December 2, 1906*

Captain Frank Hamer

Texas Ranger (1884–1955)

Captain Frank Hamer was famous for having killed Bonnie Parker and Clyde Barrow back in the early 30s. What a lot of folks don't know was he was that he had been a horseback Ranger way back in 1906 and that the first man he ever killed was Ed Putnam down in Del Rio right after he joined up. The old man had been in a slew of close up gun fights in his long and illustrious career with the Texas Rangers.

He lived in Austin after his retirement and could always be seen in the Driskill Hotel, sitting over in one of the corners of the lobby in his black suit, with his back to the wall, enjoying his morning coffee. Folks who worked there always seemed to give him a wide berth.

He and Dad were good friends and he would come out to the ranch a lot to visit. While they sat up in the living room chewing the fat, I was down in my bedroom reading about Frank and Jesse James, John Wesley Hardin and other famous gunfighters, while just about the most famous of all the Texas gunfighters to ever live, sat up in our living room. Go figure!

Dad always invited him to hunt dove on our place, and I got to see the Captain handle a shotgun. Now, all these years later, I understand why most crooks didn't want to mess with a man who could shoot like he could.

Captain Frank carried an engraved .45 Colt six-shooter, that was always stuck in the waistband of his pants. He didn't have a holster. One day I asked him to show it to me and he slipped his coat back a fraction, reached in and pulled it out for me to see. He called it "ole' Lucky."

Dad told me the old man absolutely had no fear of man nor beast. That he would walk up to an outlaw and slap the crap out of him and say, "I'm Frank Hamer." That would get your attention! After that, boys, I'm sure the gun-smoke flew. Now, that was Texas History. I'm glad I was able to witness a little bit of it out at our ranch.

When the old man died, his family asked Dad to be a pall bearer at his funeral. Dad was honored to do so. I think Dad or someone told me that when the old man died, he still had some thirteen bullets in his body from his gunfighter days.

The Kyle Years

Dad and Alice built a new ranch house about a mile east of what we call the Hays City Corner. That was near the southwest corner of the original 11,000 acres that grandfather Gil had bought in 1901. When Dad sold the 3,600-acre home pasture in 1948 to Pat Rutherford, Dad lease/purchased 1,800 acres on the south side of the original ranch from his sister, Marion K. Taylor. Aunt Marion, or Auntie, as we called her, lived over in the center of our county where she had built her home in 1933. That's when the whole ranch had been divided among the four Kuykendall children.

Along with the house, Dad built a complete processing room next door to the garage where he installed a big walk-in freezer/cooler with cutting tables, a meat block, sausage grinder and all the works to process all our own beef and particularly the wild game we killed. And so, every day or two we'd bring in the deer that had been killed that day, hang them up in a tree with a cable lift, gut them if needed, skin them, quarter them and haul all the meat into the cooler side of the locker to age for several days. After they had aged for as long as Dad thought necessary, we would process every scrap of meat on the animal. The good cuts were made into steaks or roasts and the scrap meat along the ribs and elsewhere

were cut into strips and ground to make sausage. Everything was carefully wrapped in good heavy-duty freezer paper and then frozen in the walk-in freezer. This procedure never changed. We could drive for 900 hours getting in from some far-away hunt, but when we got to the house, night or day, it was our duty to get the animals cleaned up and in the cooler side of the box before we went our separate ways.

About the time I hit sixteen or seventeen it occurred to me, if I'd quit killing so many deer, I'd have more time to chase some of those pretty girls in Kyle that were beginning to appeal to me. I wouldn't be spending so much time in the durn meat house cutting up animals. It also had become my duty to gut or clean any guest's deer and the whole process was getting to be a pain in the butt. It was getting to the point, or at least I thought, that all I did every available moment was either clean my or somebody else's damn deer. I needed to figure out how to slow the process. That's when I had one of my best hunting ideas.

Buck Fever

If you are a hunter you know what "buck fever" means. That is the simple process of becoming a complete idiot when you come face to face with a really big buck, or a little

Not Enough Bullets

one for that matter. Some folks shake like a leaf, some shuck all their shells out on the ground thinking they are shooting, while others are paralyzed with indecision.

Well, even though I have killed a zillion deer, when I ran head on into a really big buck, I could shake all the leaves out of the tree I was leaning against. So, early on it became very apparent to this young hunter that I couldn't hit a damn thing that was standing. If that sucker wasn't running or moving, I simply couldn't hold it on him. I have wrapped my arms around small trees to steady my gun and all I did was shake the bark off the tree. Therefore, it behooved me early on to let the animal start to move or run and then throw down on him and snap off a shot as I wobbled into him with my scope. Not the best of all worlds but it was all I could do.

I then decided to carry it one step further. Since I was out every single day hunting, instead of shooting at first chance, why not ease up on as many animals as I could and not shoot until, one, I had gotten as close as I could, and two, the animal had to be running. Then I carried it one more step. The shot I made had to be a neck shot. I'm here to tell you folks, if you stay with this program, and you don't have to gut so many damn deer. Man, what fun I had from then on out with the stakes so much higher.

Team Shooting

Cousin Worth and I did a lot of hunting together. He would give me a holler that he was going to make a round in his place and ask if I wanted to go with him. I'd jump in the '44 Jeep we had and run over to their part of the ranch on the other side of Onion Creek. He said he had seen a pretty

good buck down in their south pasture and he thought we might make a turn down that way and see if we could jump him. We made a big circle of the pasture. As we were going through some big live-oak motts we saw a few doe break and out came the buck he had seen. Worth bailed out of the Jeep one way and I jumped out the other, which was how we hunted. He started to jog around to get a better chance and I did the same. I hadn't run more than about fifty yards when I saw the buck break from one live-oak thicket to the next one. I slid to a stop and was getting ready to take a whack at him as soon as he broke into the clear, when he suddenly stopped and threw up his head to look at me to see what I was doing. With no hesitation I shouldered my gun and shot as soon as he appeared in my scope, shooting at the little white spot most white-tails have just under their chin. He fell like he had been pole-axed which is what happens on most neck shots. It was a hell of a shot and I was proud of myself for being able to pull it off. I started jogging up to where he had fallen and just as I approached him, I saw Worth out of the corner of my eye trotting the same way. I got to the buck before he did and was just about to say how lucky my shot was when Worth exclaimed that he had killed him. I think I said "No, you didn't, I did," or something to that effect. Worth started to argue with me so we grabbed the buck by the horns and pulled him up where we could see the shot. Lo and behold he had a hole directly in the white spot under his chin where I had shot him and another hole directly under his left ear where Worth had shot him. We had both shot at the same instant from two different locations and both made tremendous neck shots on the animal. While they were both great shots, there is also an explanation on how and why it happened the way it did. When you have hunted as much as we had, certain instincts take over in each circumstance. When the deer broke to run, I was going to wait until he hit an open spot to shoot. Then he abruptly stopped to look at me and as he did I popped him. He gave me that brief instant to react and I did. Well, think about it. Worth saw him break and he had the same reaction. Deer stops, and bang, he's dead. That was the correct reaction from two damn good hunters and pretty good shots besides. We should have mounted him with the story attached.

As I mentioned earlier, Worth had installed the 2.5 power scope on my .270, the one with the little black "Lee Dot" in the center of the cross-hairs. It was great, just jerk the gun up, put that black dot on the animal and let 'er fly. Even though we all have been guilty of sighting our guns in for long distances, mine was sighted in for two hundred yards for years even though most Hill Country shots are well below a hundred yards. Well, when the animal was out around fifty yards the little Lee Dot was fine, but at two hundred yards the durn thing just about covered the whole deer from nose to tail. That made it a tad difficult to pinpoint where the bullet was going to hit.

Wounded Animals

In all the years of our family hunting, we probably didn't lose over two or three deer. Any time an animal was wounded and got away from us, we tracked it until we found it or Dad called a friend and got him to come over to our place and bring his dogs to track for us. We didn't like to lose any venison. Every hunter worth his salt wants to make a clean kill every time he or she shoots. But when one

gets into as many fire-fights as we did occasionally things would get messy. When that happened we just went back and cleaned it up.

So, with that background, Worth called one evening and asked me to come over the next morning. He said he had wounded a little buck that afternoon and he wanted me to help him track him. I loaded our two Weimeraners, Happy and Max, in the Jeep and went over to the other ranch. Worth hopped in my Jeep and he told me he had broken the deer's right front leg. We made a big round in the part of the pasture where he thought the deer would be. We hadn't gone but about a half-mile when the little buck came busting out of a small piece of brush. Sure enough his right foreleg was busted. Well, the deer was down and across a big draw, probably 250 yards away. He started running from my right to my left and had it in pretty good gear considering he only had three legs to work with. I bailed out of the Jeep as soon as I saw him, kneeled, put the Lee Dot on him (it covered him up) and touched it off. Well, to my surprise, down he went; but then up he came again, in a dead run. Damned if I hadn't shot off the poor booger's left hind leg at the knee. Now, here he was running lickity-split using his two off legs, the left front and the right rear and bless his heart, he was pouring on the coals. Well, at my shot, both dogs came flying out of the Jeep to go get him. Worth jumped in the driver's seat and I jumped in the back so I could see which way the deer was going to run. With some difficulty and after running over a good big rock or two, we came sliding out the other side of the draw. Then Worth put the hammer down. Sure enough, there was little Mr. Buck high-tailing right down the side of the draw about seventy-five yards away. As we pulled up even with him, I tapped Worth on the shoulder to stop and he slammed on the brakes. I jerked up and tapped it to him and damned if I didn't shoot off both his horns and down he went down. Two seconds later both dogs got to him and were holding the poor little bastard down. I jumped out of the Jeep, ran down, cleared the dogs and killed him. What had started off as an attempt to find a wounded animal and put him out of his misery, ended up with me shooting off all of the poor devil's spare parts. Not at all what I had intended. But that wouldn't be the last time I shot off a set of horns.

Horn Shots

Over a period of two or three years, I shot the horns off several bucks I killed. The reason was easy: When I would swing up to shoot I was always looking at the deer's horns and my shot went where I was looking. It took me a while to realize what I was doing and took me even longer to break the habit.

Back in the earlier days when we were shooting the slow moving lead bullets of the old lever-action rifles, Dad with his .30-30 and me with my .25-20, a deer hit in the horns might get knocked down or turned around but usually it wouldn't kill him. But when we all migrated into the higher velocities, like my .270 and Dad's .300 Weatherby in the early 1950s, things changed. If you shot the buck through the tips of his horns you'd usually stagger him pretty good but if you shot him through the base of his horns you'd kill him as dead as a hammer.

The first thing you'd see would be a big puff of white smoke, just as if you'd shot through a five-pound sack of flour. The next instant you'd see Mr. Buck going ass-over-tea-kettle, and the third thing you might see were little bitty pieces of horn about fifty

feet up in the air. About that time, you'd think, damn, guess I can't nail those horns up on the wall.

I will assure you that a .270 bullet traveling about 2,800 feet per second and Dad's .300 traveling about 3,500 to 4,000 feet per second will blow all the hair off an ole' buck if you hit him low down in the horns.

Shoot 'Em in the Neck

I never hunted turkeys even though we had lots of them. That's because you can't walk up on a turkey. Since we didn't have deer stands in those days, it was just a matter of shooting at them when you saw them. So, since I mainly hunted afoot, I'd shoot at 'em when I'd see them but it was a waste of good bullets. One day I had taken the Jeep down to our east fence line, parked it, and was easing along down toward the creek, when a big gobbler gobbled at me and flew right over my head. I un-slung my trusty shooting iron and let fly at him just as he went over me. The feathers flew and down he came. Well, how many turkeys have you shot in the butt with a .270? There's nothing left but a pile of goo surrounded by turkey feathers. The shot was automatic. If you're dumb enough to fly over my head, I'm gonna shoot at-cha. Your mistake!

Well, you won't believe my surprise when I walked up to the gobbler and rolled him over. Instead of a big mess, he was completely intact. I looked closer and my bullet had entered the soft spot right behind his right wing and had come out the sticking place and the damn bullet never broke up. So, that was my first turkey; and a hell of a wing shot if I may say so myself.

Let's go back to my change of tactics about neck shooting. I had gone down to the same locale, crossed Onion Creek, looked around, hadn't seen anything and had re-crossed the creek. Just as I topped the bluff, who should be standing in the middle of the road but Mr. Buck himself, and a damn good one at that. As I usually did when I had the Jeep, I had both dogs, Happy and Max with me. I instantly jammed the gear in low, cut the engine and stepped out. Well, the ole' buck was so surprised he just stood there all fuzzed up. He bobbed his head like he wanted to fight and I could see his hair was standing up. It was obvious he didn't really know what or who I was so I started easing toward him. He was only about fifty steps from me. Now, when something like this happens, I am bowed up like a tomcat getting ready for a fight. After about ten very slow and careful yards and me actually yelling at him to run, Mr. Buck blew up and turned wrong-side-out. When he whirled and broke straight away from me, I snapped up and popped him right in the back of the neck. Then, for an instant, nothing happened. Instead of going down like he'd been hit with a sledgehammer he kept running like nothing had happened. I was reaching over to shuck in another shell when he suddenly went head over heels in a cloud of dust. It was like a slight time warp. Bang, one, two, three, and then over he went. While I was putting in another shell, up he comes on his hinds legs, with his head and fore-end still on the ground, pushing himself around. Then, like a light switch being turned off and on, he did this two or three more times. By that time, my trusty warriors, Happy and Max, who had been as patient as they could, were on him like ugly on ape.

In those days, the first thing you did when you got up on a buck was cut his throat. That was just the way we always did it. If he got up and ran, he wouldn't run far. So, I wrestled him down, trying to push the dogs out of the way, and cut his throat. It was then I saw what had happened. The bullet had struck him on the left side of his neck, going forward, and had blown off about six or eight inches of his neck, all the way down to his vertebra. He was going from being paralyzed to not, and in between, he'd try to jump up and run off. It was all I could do to get him in the back of the Jeep. He tried to kick his way out even after I got him in the back. He was one tough customer. The shot I made was typical of my shots until the "Kuykendall Shot" was developed and made famous.

Brother Gil and Friends

During this period as I was attempting to adhere to my new shooting and stalking habits, my brother Gil would show up from the big university in Austin with some of his buddies. Gil was one of the best young golfers in the US of A and had worked hard and gotten on the University of Texas golf team in the late 40s. Harvey Penick was his coach. Turns out, the golf team and the football team all lived together in Hill Hall, just across the street from the stadium. One of Gil's many buddies was Tom Stolhandske, one of the best All-American ends who ever played for Texas. Sure enough, Gil showed up at the ranch one day with Tom and asked if I'd take him on a tour. I, of course, was happy to oblige.

I cranked up the Jeep without the dogs and we made a round down along Onion Creek to see what might jump out and scare us. We got to a spot where a game trail I liked veered off to the right and went up on the bluff. I cut the Jeep off and motioned to Tom to follow me and we eased up that way. As we slipped along up the trail I motioned to Tom to be very quiet, follow real close and to do exactly as I did. I stopped, he stopped, I went, he went. We hadn't gone but about fifty yards when I peeked over the edge of the bluff and saw a little buck lying down about fifteen to twenty steps in front of me. He had his eyes closed while chewing his cud. I froze, Tom froze. He didn't know what was taking place. I very carefully reached behind me without ever taking my eyes off the buck, got a hold of Tom's sleeve, and very quietly pulled him up along side me until he could see the deer. He then stuck the .30-30 up by me so the barrel was beyond me, and touched it off. Killed that sucker dead. Mr. Buck never knew what hit him. Tom was thrilled. He didn't realize he had just experienced one of the best hunting stalks of his life. Sometimes you get lucky.

Getting Up Close

That area of our ranch was a favorite of mine because Onion Creek meandered through it and there were several nice cuts and arroyos that fed into the creek—great sneaking areas for a walk hunter like yours truly. One morning, I got out just after day break and drove the Jeep just short of the water crossing on the main road over to Aunt Dorothy's. I piled out and started easing along the grassy bank. The grass was still damp from the dew and I liked that, since it cut down on the noise a bunch. Walking in the afternoon after everything dried out made a crunching sound as you walked but in the early part of the day that noise was eliminated. Also, unless it was real cold I always wore a deerskin shirt and this was a great help.

A walk hunter is always easing through different kinds of brush, small cedars, per-

simmon, algerita and such and anything that scrapped along a cloth jacket would make a little tiny scratching sound. That was very distracting to me, because I always wanted to be completely silent. I did not make any noise at all when I did this. I would ease along, slowly, looking constantly around me to see what might be looking at me. Most wild animals don't react to color, they react to movement. Anyway, this was way before anyone started using the bright orange that is required in present day hunts in most states.

But I didn't trust anything, clothes or color, so I always wore my leather and dressed as neutral as I could so I'd blend in with the country side. Many times when I'd spot a deer, it would see me at the same moment. I would freeze and stay in whatever position I was in until the deer looked away. Foot up in the air, head turned, didn't matter what, I froze. Sometimes it might take a few seconds, sometimes it might take a minute or two.

A Cow in the Woods

Try holding your foot in the air for a minute, sure will give you a hell of a cramp. If the deer hadn't boogered right away, usually I was all right. As soon as the animal dropped its head and started to graze, I'd lower my foot, freeze, and let it look at me again. It would soon drop its head again and then I'd squat. By squatting usually you would get out of its line of sight. So, in about an hour I had made about a half-mile. There were several cuts or draws coming in from the left and I kinda wanted to get into one of them and work my way out on top. That way I could reverse my course and work my way back to the Jeep to conclude my morning sojourn.

I had just started up one of the cuts when I started picking up a strange light popping or crunching sound. Seemed like it was in front of me and up the draw but it took a while before I could figure out where it was coming from. It was obviously an animal eating something. Now, one of the worse things that can happen to a walk hunter is to ease up on a damn cow. She'll see you and want to know what in the hell you are. By the time she gets through running around through the brush and timber trying to decide, she has run everything off in the entire pasture and your hunt is ruined for that day. So, I tried very hard not to let Mrs. Cow ever see me.

Stalking a Popping Sound

I walked up the draw a hundred or hundred-fifty yards before I topped out on the level area above. I eased along, still hearing that strange noise every few seconds and finally realized it was up ahead of me and slightly to my left. It seemed like forever, straining with each step not to make a single sound, before I finally got to the crest. Now, when Dad had cleared this part of the ranch of its cedar, he cut a *sendero* (opening) along the bluff line so we could ride our horses there without being completely in the brush. That is what I was getting ready to step into, still hearing the sound. There were several scrub cedars scattered along in the road-like clearing with a fairly decent sized one about twenty to thirty steps to my left that was covered with cedar-berries. I froze as I stuck my head out in the opening to get a peek, looking both ways. Then I took about a half-step out and froze again. Whatever the sound was, it was coming from the cedar bush in front of me that was full of berries. I must have stood there two or three minutes without moving a muscle, straining to hear better and never taking

my eyes off that bush. Finally I moved two steps, then two more steps, when I saw something at ground level on the other side of the tree that did not look right. I stared at it for a bit and suddenly realized I was seeing was the right front foot of a deer that had its head in that damn cedar tree. It was eating the hell out of those berries and that was what the popping and crunching sound had been all along. Turns out the animal was directly on the other side, facing me, with the thick cedar tree completely obscuring its view of me. There was nothing to do but go and investigate.

It must have taken me fifteen minutes to cover those few yards, but the deer was so intent on eating those damn berries, that I was able to make it all the way to the tree, undiscovered. By this time, I had my .270 at the ready, which means in both hands. As I got to the tree, I eased the rifle into my left hand with the safety off. I was holding it like a pistol around the grip area. With my finger on the trigger, I reached carefully up with my right hand and very, very, gently pulled a limb back where I could see what in the hell it was, all the time swinging that nine pound rifle up to get ready to shoot. About that time a little six-point buck suddenly realized he was no longer all by his lonesome, and popped his head around there to see who or what it was. When he saw me his eyes got just about as big as two of Alice's pie pans and that was the last thing he remembered. So, long story short, I guess about four feet is the closest I ever got to a deer before I killed him.

Alice's Deer Skin Gloves

Back during the Great War, Mother started making deer-skin gloves. I mention this because when Dad got ready to go to Canada in 1947, she made him a fringed leather shirt to hunt in and while she was at it, she made me one, too. She figured I must be part Indian anyway. So, from that day for many, many years, I wore that shirt every time I went to hunt. With my fancy fringed shirt tucked into my best Levis, which were then tucked into my beat-up Red Wing boots, and my trusty .270 hanging over my shoulder I was quite a sight to behold.

When Mother decided she wanted to make the gloves, she got Dad and everyone to save her the deer hides off the animals that were killed. When they reached about 100, Dad would salt them down, box them up, take them into the railroad depot at Buda and ship them to some place in Wisconsin to a tanning factory. Mother got so good at it and so well known during the war years that she had customers all over the country. This happened because Dad had played polo all over the southwest on up into Cleveland and when their friends found out what she was doing, everyone wanted a pair of deer-skin gloves from the Kuykendall Ranch in Buda, Texas. It wasn't long until Neiman-Marcus in Dallas and the Lucchese Boot Company in San Antonio were handling her wares. She cut the patterns and hand stitched hundreds of pairs over the years and didn't stop until we moved to the south side of the ranch in 1948. She told me later on that she had ruined the muscles in her right arm pushing and pulling the needle through that tough leather all those years. I think it is now called Carpel Tunnel Syndrome.

The South Side of the Ranch

As mentioned earlier, Dad had been friends with LaVerne Allen for years. When we moved to the south side of the ranch,

I was able to move back home and attend Kyle High School as a junior. LaVerne Allen's son, David LaVerne, also went there and we became friends for life. There were very few kids going to that school in those days. In fact, they were only able to suit-up a six-man football team. Being a new warm body, it was expected that I participate, so I threw my 130-pound self into the melee.

David LaVerne loved hunting as much as I did. He lived west of Kyle on a part of the old Nance ranch that fronted the beautiful Blanco River, and it was a lot of fun for me to stay at his place, I spent many wonderful days wandering the woods with him.

He and I were so involved in our old guns, that in 1950, we decided to join the newly formed Texas Gun Collectors Association which met once a year at the fancy Shamrock Hotel in Houston. I think it cost us $20 to join. He was number 420 and I was number 421. We went for a year or two until college and the military intervened and life got different for a while. We'd drive to Houston, taking some old rusty gun with the barrel sawed off and think we were in hog heaven. Man, was that a sight, tables and tables full of nothing but antique guns. We had a blast. That was back during the time that no one was allowed into the gun show with anything that that was not an authentic antique. The door keepers would inspect all entries and nothing else was allowed. Those early gun shows were nothing like those today, where a bunch of pot-bellied old boys, dressed in full camouflage and spitting in their coffee cans, come in bringing the latest and best machine-gun as if they getting ready to invade Mexico.

David and I both had traded for several muzzle-loading rifles and were constantly down along the Blanco River taking a pot-shot at something. We had on our leather shirts, our powder horns and our "possibles bag" over our shoulders. The bags held all the goodies necessary for the outing, lead balls, cloth patches, and other black powder paraphernalia. Man, we were ready for Indians, animals or whatever might decide to attack us that particular day. Those were fun times.

Muzzle-Loader Hunting

In keeping with this grand tradition, I decided I'd better get into the woods up at our place and see if I could kill a deer with my .39 caliber percussion rifle. I had gotten it from an old man out of Fort Stockton, Texas who was a big muzzle-loader shooter back in those days. He had bored it out from about a .30 caliber to the .39, and had been shooting targets with it for several years when I got it. I think he won some competitive shooting event in West Texas one year with it. The rifle was about five feet long or so, and was what most people refer to as a Kentucky rifle, full stocked all the way to the end of the octagon barrel. Underneath the barrel was a hickory ramrod that you used to pack the powder and ball down the barrel when you loaded it. Took several minutes to complete the whole process and was quite cumbersome if you didn't hold your mouth right.

I, very carefully, put all the paraphernalia in the Jeep one day, left the dogs at home, and went down along Potter Creek to become a better frontiersman than I already was. I parked the Jeep down along Potter Spring and started easing up the hill above it. There was a little opening up on top where I figured I could sit for a while and see if something might come by me. Well, I hadn't been there thirty minutes when this little four-pointer came sashaying by me without

MEK and David L. Allen
Frontiersmen

a care in the world. I swung up and shot him way back in the floating rib, which is the last rib on an animal before you shoot him in the guts. It was a terrible shot for a bunch of reasons. One, the damn gun would key-hole at a hundred yards and he was about thirty steps from me, and two, since he hadn't seen me I had plenty of time and didn't have to hurry my shot. So, what in the heck was I doing shooting him in the middle of the body like that? Well, when I popped him, the little tiny bullet went plum through him and lodged against his hide on the far side. He didn't know what had happened and for a bit neither did I. All the buck knew was something had lightly tapped his side, so he stood there for the longest time trying to figure it all out. In the mean time, yours truly, is now lying

37

Not Enough Bullets

flat on my back so the damn deer can't see me, trying to recharge that five-foot-long muzzle-loading rifle. And, for some reason, black powder won't pour down a rifle lying sideways, so unless one stands and pours it from the top, you ain't gonna get it reloaded. It was a hell of a dilemma.

I don't know how long it took, though it seemed like hours. By the time I finally squirmed around and got the damn thing loaded again, the poor little buck just went over, lay down and died. God, it was pitiful. So, even though I had my picture taken after I got him home that day, I decided it was in the best interest of history not to tell very many folks what actually happened. I cleaned up that little rifle and never hunted with it again after that day.

Danger in the Woods

Dad was a hell of a woodsman and he had some real peculiar habits when he'd shoot a big buck back in the early days when he was still using his .30-30. Hunting in the Texas Hill Country is completely different than hunting in South Texas. First place, a big South Texas buck will hook the hell out of you if you wound him and are not careful how you approach him, where a Hill Country buck is not so inclined. I think it has a lot to do with where the animal was raised. If it was born and reared in the deep brush country of South Texas where there were plenty of mountain lions, a deer didn't get to be several years old without having a hell of a fight or two to survive.

So, Dad taught me early on, when you've shot and knocked down a big buck and started to track him down and ease up on him, be very careful. If his eyes were shut, shoot that son of a gun again, and shoot him quick, 'cause he's not dead. And for God's sake,

MEK with muzzle loader and buck

don't ease up and poke him in the butt with a stick or your gun barrel. He's lying there waiting to get his bearings and when you poke him to see if he will flinch, I'm here to tell you, he will. And you won't like it one bit. If he's dead, normally his eyes will be open, unless of course, he turns and looks at you. Then, I'm sure you can figure that one out without me having to tell you.

Another thing Dad would do after he had a deer down, was step over behind his head, reach down and jerk one foreleg up and over the buck's horns on that side. I asked him what in the world he did that for? He said, "You jerk that foot up over that horn and he can never get up and hook you." In Africa, I've been told, when the Great White Hunter shoots a big cape buffalo, the first thing the tracker does is ease in behind the animal and

Bill Kuykendall—Cowboy

slice his tendons on both rear legs. Why? So, he can't get up! Strange habits, but all come from long practice of having really weird things happen to you when you are out in the boonies all by your lonesome.

Roping the Buck
or
Rodeo in the South Pasture

Dad was a real cowboy. If anything got too close to him, he was gonna rope it. I never could rope worth a durn, but Dad could rope

anything. He usually rode a big, black stud horse named Smooth Sailing. Smooth was the horse he had used in the late 30s on his polo tours and that stud would do anything Dad asked him to do. Dad could rope a goat off of him or the biggest Brahman bull you ever saw and jerk that son of a gun flat as a pancake.

One day he was moseying down in the front pasture on old Smooth and just as he broke clear of a little batch of cedar a good buck came busting out right by him. With no hesitation Dad laid about fourteen pounds of spur into ole' Smooth and in about eight big jumps, daubed it on him. Roping with a

Not Enough Bullets

small loop is good for goats, sheep, and the like, but it would have been helpful if the loop had cleared his buck's horns and settled around his neck. Dad could then have jerked him around until he choked his eyeballs out, but he caught the top of the deer's horns instead. He told me later about the third time that buck hit the end of that thirty-foot rope, it did a double back-flip and broke back under old Smooth. That's when the real rodeo commenced. No matter how gentle or well trained your pony is, a deer running under you with that roping-rope is rather disconcerting.

How Dad was able to stay on that bucking horse with that deer hitting the end of the rope at the same time has to be another tale. But, the end of this story seems to be that somewhere through the dust and the smoke of the event, Dad was able to get that damn rope off his saddle. "I just let that son of a bitch have it," he later said.

I Never Change Guns

My gun and I have been together for many, many years and we have experienced lots of good times together and several real wrecks. When I see something I need to shoot there is never any hesitation. I unravel my gun and when it hits my shoulder it's gonna go off. There is no aiming because I shoot with both eyes open and when the gun comes up I already see the deer. If I ask you to suddenly point your finger at an object you can see what I am telling you. Try it.

Also, I never change the type of guns I shoot. I have shot the same style of Winchester all of my life. It has the same safety mechanism and using it is completely natural for me. I don't even realize I am taking the gun off safety as it starts toward my shoulder, it just happens. Also, all my extra

guns were pre-war. I am left handed and the Tilden Safety is featured on all Model 70 Winchesters made in the 1930s. So, for all my regular hunts, I had my spare .270 and for bigger hunts in later years, my spare was a Model 70 in the .300 H&H caliber. All my gun stocks would have the same measurement from the trigger to the rear. I could blindfold myself, pull any gun out of a scabbard and shoot it with out experiencing any changes. Of course, the kick might be a little different. That .300 and later, a .375 H&H do have the tendency to make all your gold fillings fall out of your teeth.

The Three-to-Five Count

Which brings me around to the subject of a three-to-five count? I want you to count "one thousand and one, one thousand and two…" up to five. It doesn't matter if I am in the Jeep, in the pickup, walking or watching a Chi-chi bird fly by, whatever, when that deer appears, I will get my shot off before a five-count. This comes, not from training, as much as it comes from competition. Let me explain.

My father was a rough and tumble rancher and a hell of a hunter. He wasn't really into kids. My brother and I appeared into this world back in the late '20s and early '30s and Dad just had to live with it. One way to deal with it was to send us off to boarding houses and boarding schools in hopes we'd never come back. Well, it worked with my brother, Gil. He was sent off so much he just stayed away. Not me, I wanted to be a rancher, so I squalled and bawled until they let me live at home, some time. So, as I got old enough to hunt, Dad reluctantly taught me the do's and don'ts of the sport. But down deep he was a very competitive person. No one could out-rope him, out-Polo him or out-shoot him, certainly not some piss-ant kid. It was all right when I was little, but when I hit about 16 or 17 and got pretty good, the rules changed.

Competition Shooting

Dad always drove the Jeep or the pickup when we went hunting. If it was the pickup and we had a guest, I had to sit in the middle and the guest got the door. Dad would see a good buck, stop the pickup where it was to his advantage, and get out while the guest was fumbling with the door handle. He'd then shoot at the deer before we could get ready. The same rules applied when we were by ourselves. It would make you get in a hurry.

Now, let's take the Jeep. It had no top and we hunted with the windshield down. Dad would see a buck, turn the Jeep so he could get the first shot and I had to scramble for myself. If we had a guest, the guest got to sit in the front right hand seat and I got to sit or stand in the back. I usually stood and held on to the roll bar. When Dad saw a deer, he went through his routine: He'd slow the vehicle down by throwing it in first gear and turning the key off. The Jeep would commence to stutter, stumble and jump. Just before it shuttered to a complete stop, I would have my butt over the side, break to the rear, whirl and try and maybe get a shot off before Dad could. He thought that was hilarious.

You see Dad was right handed, so all he had to do was turn the vehicle slightly to the right and either shoot out the pickup window or if in the Jeep, just shoot. Being left handed it took me a wee-bit more work. After about two years of this kind of training, I got where I could either match his shot or beat him and the battle was on.

Let me tell you a funny story. Dad, a guest and I were over in the flats driving the Jeep along between several big live oak motts when out piled about five or ten doe, yearlings and probably three or four little bucks of various sizes. It was a clear, cool, beautiful day, the birds were chirping and the grass was blowing in the breeze. The guest was taking it all in, having a fine time, when all of a sudden Dad guns the Jeep for about forty yards, whirls the wheel to the right and turns the key off. Falling or jumping out all in one motion, he then commences to shoot. Well, unbeknown to the guest, who had his rifle in his hands, the war had begun and he didn't know the rules of the game. I was already out and I'm here to tell you inside of a three-or-four count we had three of the four bucks down. The guest, whose eyes were about as big as a pie pans, was wondering what in holy hell had just taken place. He was so dumbfounded he couldn't speak for a moment or two. Meanwhile, Dad and I were grinning like two Cheshire cats over a canary, wondering why the poor son of a gun was so slow. Welcome to the club.

We Never Shoot Forward

We had certain do's and don'ts of hunting in an open Jeep. The folks in the two front seats can shoot straight forward or around to 90 degrees. Let me translate. If you are driving, you can basically shoot straight ahead or around to your left to about the 90-degree mark. It is just the reverse if you are in the right front seat. Now, if I was in the back and still in the vehicle, I could never shoot forward. You can lean as far forward as the roll bar will let you, stretch out as much as you can, and if you shoot forward even after doing all that, you will blow the hats off the folks in the front seats and they will be deaf for a week. And, on top of that, my father would chew your ass out royally and deservedly so. So, if the deer was in front and I was in the back, I'd bail out while the Jeep was still moving and run about ten steps to one side or the other and hope I could get a shot in before my dad did. If not, as he put it, "That was tough."

R.O.W.

We developed a "right of way" system for our hunting. If you are in the back of a vehicle, the people in the front always have the right of way. Whatever they do or wherever they go, the person in the rear must give way or make allowances. The person in the rear can not shoot by them or close to them, same principal as shooting forward in a Jeep. It is a No-No. So, if you are in the rear, not only do you have to be fast, you have to move out of the way for your shot because safety should take precedent over everything. If you use this same principle when you are shooting doves over a dirt tank you will never shoot someone else in the face with birdshot.

These practices came from years and years of hard and fast shooting and were designed around action and safety combined. Luckily for us, in all our years together, we never had a close call nor was anyone ever hurt because of our handling of guns. I say luckily, hell, it wasn't luck. It was because we were damn good.

Not Enough Bullets

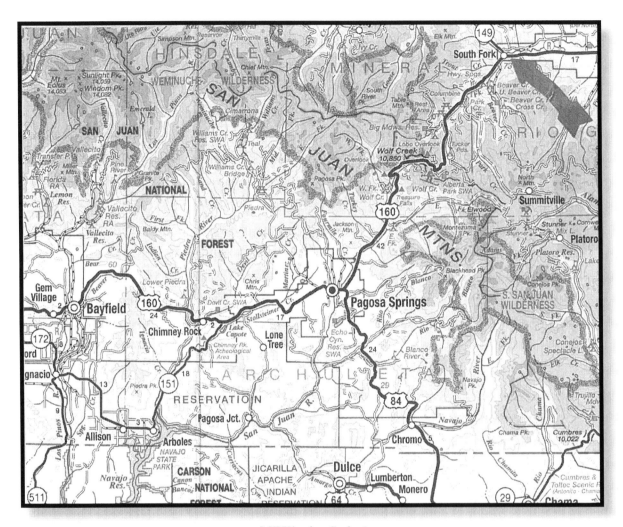

MEK's 1st Safari
South Fork, Colorado—1949

My First High Country Hunt

One of the first big hunts I got to go on was in the fall of 1949. One of Dad's buddies from down around Nixon, Texas, James Jennings, moved his whole family up to South Fork, Colorado. That fall, he decided to backpack into the big mountains around Wolf Creek Pass for an Elk hunt; and whistled at Dad to see if he wanted to get some friends together and come up for his first hunt. Dad did. He told me I could go: so I approached Mrs. Charles Wallace, the principal of "Dear ole' Kyle High," to get permission. She figured the school might be a lot safer and quieter for at least *that* week, and told me I could go.

Dad invited his brother, Ike, from Dripping Springs, along with several others, and off we went to the high country. Jennings had bought a little motel on the Wolf Creek Pass side of South Fork and that's where we unloaded all our stuff and spent the first night in preparation for our Colorado "safari."

Most general hunting seasons out west start around October 1. That's also about the same time the weather gets very unpredictable in the southern to central Rockies as the fall equinox passes. We were about to experience some of those changes.

Early the following morning, we hustled out of the motel at the crack of dawn and started to help with all the pack horses. There

were around fifteen horses, and there were eight folks. We had to have enough horses to ride and to pack in all our tents, food, and gear. Here we were coming out of Central Texas, where I'm sure it was probably 80 degrees, and this particular morning there was "frost on the pumpkin aplenty." It was great. We all got away by mid-morning and it took us the entire day to get up above the pass, which is about 10,000 feet, and into a beautiful little meadow area where our main camp was planned. There was a mountain stream nearby and the scenery was out of this world; a perfect place to start. We got our tents unloaded and set up, a big crackling fire going and started a pot of stew. That was Dad's specialty. He had killed a mule deer yearling on the way in, already had it skinned out, cut up and in the pot.

By nightfall, everything was in place like we'd been there forever. James' son and I were the only youngsters on the hunt. So we sat around, enthralled with all the tales of hunts past that the older folks were spinning. The night grew darker, the weather got colder, the fire got warmer and for the oldsters, the whiskey got better.

The next morning arrived, clear and cold. Young Jennings and I got our horses saddled and were off on our own for the day. We hunted several miles from camp by riding on established trails, stopping every now

Not Enough Bullets

and then to glass an area or two, and then proceed on our way. We were simply making a big loop that would eventually circle back into camp. We had stopped for lunch, tied our horses, and were making just a brief walk hunt when we jumped several elk cows and yearlings.

It was legal to shoot cows or yearlings in those years so the race was on. I broke off to one side and caught a glimpse of the herd running from my left to my right. From experience, I knew one could not swing and shoot in dense timber without hitting every single tree in the forest. So, I swung ahead of the bunch until I found a little bitty open spot where I thought they'd cross, and held it for just a moment. An instant later, I saw a nose then fur in my scope and I fired. Turns out, one of the long yearlings was in the lead and sure enough, I hit him and down he went. We were ecstatic.

My *compadre* and I then got to work cleaning the animal, a job that took us about an hour. We rolled him over so he would drain, then rolled him on his back and covered him with spruce bows. This would allow his cavity to cool over night, which would keep it from spoiling. The spruce limbs were there to keep the Magpies away. I didn't know that the beautiful black and white Magpies were meat eaters and any game left uncovered would be eaten down to the hair. We then gathered up our horses and made it back into camp just at dusk to give our report. Several others in the group had gotten into a herd of cows and several cows were killed, so the hunt was starting off on a very positive note.

That night, Dad and Mr. Jennings thought it would be a good idea if we two went back over to my kill with two pack horses the next morning, cut up my animal, and took the meat back down the mountain to the motel. It would serve two purposes. We had a list of stuff that Dad wanted. So, not only could we get my kill down the mountain, we could get some supplies that they felt were needed. It would be a two day trek, one to do our job and get down, and one day to get back.

So bright and early the next morning, we set out on our quest. The day turned out very cloudy and looked like rain or snow. We got to the animal a little before noon and started skinning him out. We had taken a meat saw, so once we had him where we could handle him, we quartered him using the meat saw and heaved him onto the packs we had on the two pack horses. It was all we could do to get that booger loaded. The weather had worsened all morning and by midday when we finally got all the meat packed, the snow fell so hard we couldn't see our horse's heads. We swung on our horses and started to try and find the main trail down the mountain. We were in more danger than we knew because young Jennings didn't have a clue where we were and I sure as hell didn't. I didn't even know which state I was in, much less which way was up or down.

As luck would have it, I had been in the Army/Navy store in Austin a week or so before looking at all their World War II surplus stuff and came upon a military compass that caught my eye. Knowing I was going to be in the "wilds of the west," I bought it and just happened to have that little sucker in my coat pocket. It saved our bacon! When I dug that thing out of my coat pocket after an hour or so and got it open, I saw we were headed northwest when we needed to be riding southeast. We had been going deeper and deeper into the black timber and didn't know it. I'm not saying we would have died or anything, but we certainly would have had a different tale to tell when and if we survived.

After we realized our dilemma, we reversed course, and very late that afternoon stumbled on to the main trail that took us down the mountain to the motel. We got there right at dark, wet to the skin and damn near frozen to our saddles. We were mighty glad to see civilization, not to mention having a great supper and a steaming hot bath.

The following day, we awoke to clear sky, about ten degrees above zero and a foot or two of snow in the lower elevations. We did our duty, got whatever extra goods were needed, and were back in camp by that nightfall. The snow at the higher elevation was about two feet on the flats and much deeper in the drifts. Quite an experience.

Never Eat Yellow Snow

I very seldom drank water in the winter time. I think I had started drinking coffee by then but that was all. I just don't get thirsty in the winter time. Different metabolism I guess, I have no other explanation. But the habit saved my life on that Colorado hunt. Turns out everyone else in camp drank plenty of water all the time, and they were drinking it out of that pure, flowing stream right by our camp. You would, too. The stream was right there and it was beautiful. Just go down and dip your tin cup into it and have at it. As luck will have it, there is some sort of bug that lives in all those gorgeous streams that I think comes from elk poop and "it do not like humans." On about the fourth day everyone except me came down

with parasitic dysentery, which is known in the ranching country as "the scours." It is combined with a statement that is closely associated with *"OH, SHIT."* Now, in case you are sensitive to the language, have you ever in your whole born days heard someone jump up in the middle of the night and mutter, *"OH, DYSENTERY?"* I didn't think so.

About midnight, the night of our return, I was awakened in my tent by every single person uttering a similar country version of the above statement, combined with the rustling sound of them tearing out of their bedrolls, jerking open the tent flap, then a rapid, crunch, crunch, crunch, through the deep snow and then, well, you know the sound.

When I got up the next morning, every one in camp but me was sick. There was no coffee made, so I went over to the cook tent to get something started. I noticed all those foot prints in the snow going in all directions, and at the end of each set of prints was a little round, brown stain in the snow, which I'd rather not discuss. I think somewhere later in life I read something that said, "Never eat yellow snow." I guess no one ever figured a warning about brown snow was necessary.

All I remember about the rest of the hunt was that everyone remained in camp that whole next day. The following day, we broke camp, and with Dad in the lead walking to break the snow, we made our way off the mountain. When we got home, my six-man football team needed all the help it could get; with me gone there were only ten boys out for the team that year. So, I put the experience of my first safari behind me and once again became a useful Kyle Panther.

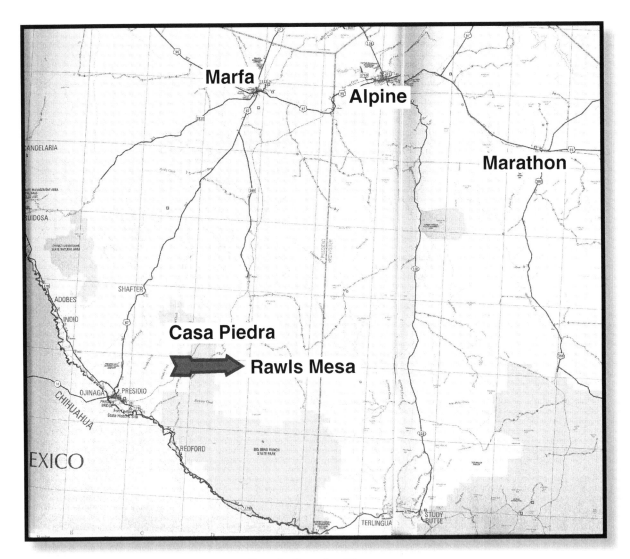

Rawls Ranch—Texas

Rawls Ranch

The West Texas Years
The Rawls and the Mitchells

The summer of 1949 brought with it the realization that if I wanted to go to college anywhere, I'd better start trying to figure it out. So, that summer Dad and I drove out to Alpine, Texas for me to take a peek at Sul Ross State College. I always wanted to be a rancher and I wanted to go to a good ranching college. I didn't want to go to a big school like Texas A&M, and since Sul Ross had one of the best range management schools in the state, I chose it. Another reason might have been that Dad had a bunch of old friends in the Alpine-Marfa area. They had gone to school with him at South West Normal in the 1910s at San Marcos, Texas. The name was later changed to Southwest Texas State Teachers College.

Dad's friend in that high country was Joe Mitchell. He and his family are very well known in the Davis Mountains region of West Texas. And so, we were about to enter the most important phase of my hunting life, the West Texas years.

Dad and I drove out there that summer and probably spent a week getting acquainted with the school and his old friends over at Marfa. During our visit Mitchell decided to take us down to the Rawls ranch. Turns out he hunted down there with that family and he wanted Dad to get to know them. He also had extended an invitation for us to join him on a hunt the following year after I had started college.

The Rawls ranch, or Rawls Mesa, as I call it, was forty or fifty miles southeast of Marfa. We went straight south of Marfa on the Presidio highway for about six miles and then angled off to the left on what is known as the Casa Piedra Road. As soon as we turned off the highway, the ranch road became dirt and we drove for what seemed like an eternity down that old dusty road until we spotted a sharp peak in front of us, called San Jacinto Mountain. We went through a series of cattle guards and as we approached the peak itself, you could see this distinct, high mesa just beyond it. "That is where we are going," Mitchell told Dad. So we went by San Jacinto Peak and right up to the base of the mesa, which now towered 300 or 400 feet over our heads. At that point, we came to the locked gate with a bullet-perforated sign nailed to a fence post that said "Rawls Ranch-No Trespassing!" I almost laughed, 'cause it seemed like you'd have to drive 10,000 miles and have lots of drinking water even to have found the ranch, much less trespass on it.

We entered the ranch through a big canyon and soon worked our way out on top of the mesa, where you could see for a hundred miles in every direction. It was, and is, very spectacular. We drove about another half an hour or so just to get to the ranch headquarters. The ranch covered close to 60,000

Not Enough Bullets

San Jacinto Peak & Road to Rawls Ranch

Rawls Ranch Entrance

acres and we were just on one edge. After opening five or six gates, we arrived at the Rawls headquarters and were met by Jack Rawls, who had just flown in from Marfa to meet us in his little Air Coupe.

In 1949 all three of the Rawls men were still alive: Grandpa Tom Rawls, who was probably seventy or so; his son, Jack, who met us, and was probably fifty and Jack's son Jack Jr., who everyone called Junie. He was around thirty.

What struck me immediately about all these men, including Mitchell, was how little bitty they were. All of them were about five-six or five-seven, thin as a split rail, and all had on their little Stetson hats and about size seven Lucchese cowboy boots. They wore long-sleeved shirts and Levi pants and were all dried up and grizzled from living their whole lives in the great Chihuahuan Desert. Their faces were like burnt toast and they had that look that made you think all the moisture had been sucked out of them a long time ago.

Our relationship with this family began that summer day and would last for the rest of their lives. Jack and Junie welcomed me to West Texas, congratulated me on coming out to attend such a fine college and turned to my father and told him he should come hunt with them after I started school. This started our West Texas hunting adventures on that ranch, a run that would last eighteen years.

The Rawls ranch had three divisions. The largest was the Tascatal, the 30,000-acre main headquarters, where Jack, Sr. stayed when he came out from town. Next, was the 22,000-acre Holquin, where Junie and his wife lived. The Holquin was not far from the main gate we had come through. Finally, there was the 10,000-acre Alazan. That's where Grandpa Tom Rawls stayed

when he came out from Marfa. The Alazan, which means *sorrel horse* in Spanish, was off the mesa in a big canyon back on the east side of the ranch. In fact, when Grandpa Rawls drove out to the ranch in his old black two-door pickup, he didn't have to come up on top of the mesa like we did, he could go by San Jacinto Peak, hook a left and drive underneath the mesa rim until he got to the Alazan canyon. There, he had an old ranch house, a set of working pens, a big windmill and a concrete storage tank for water. I only went down there one time in all those years, because we were not allowed to hunt down there.

Junie Rawls

Not Enough Bullets

Junie Rawls Holguin house

Sul Ross State College and the Rawls Ranch

Six-man football came and went that fall of 1949 at Kyle High. All nine of us seniors went flying into our last semester struggling to pass all our classes so we could graduate that coming May 1950. I am not sure my grades were all that good, but Mrs. Wallace had had about all my shenanigans she could stand in one life time. I suspect she rigged my grades just to get me *out of there*. I was much obliged.

Some time later that summer, my folks took me to San Antonio, where I boarded the train for Alpine. It was my first time riding a train and I rode that beast out to West Texas where I was to begin a new life, for a while.

I know Dad came out for the hunt at the ranch that November, but I have no memory

of it. What I do remember is that the next year, 1951, Dad had talked the Rawls into leasing him the hunting rights to the ranch. Dad made a deal with them to bring out ten or fifteen hunters who would pay the Rawls family a small amount, probably less than $50 a person. You have to remember, hunting leases were practically unheard of in Texas in 1950. All that would change in later years, becoming a multi-billion dollar industry. The main reason is that Texas is a private property state. Translated, that means there are very few public places to hunt in Texas. If you want to hunt in Texas, you have to pay the land owner for that right.

When we first saw the Rawls ranch, there were only a few roads and those led to the different houses or the few water wells and windmills on the place. Most of the ranch

Rawls Ranch

work was done on horseback and so no extensive network of roads had been built. Consequently, when we went hunting, it was by foot. Dad or someone would drive out a ranch road until it ended at a windmill or water-well, pile everybody out and tell you what time he'd pick you up that afternoon.

Cousin Worth came out the second year and he's the one who started our practice of "trotting." He'd get out of a vehicle, get his rifle in his hand and off he'd go in a high lope with little puffs of dust popping up from his boots. Soon, he'd be out of sight. Well, I would be right behind him. Face it, that ranch was so big that to get anywhere worth hunting, you had to travel ten or fifteen miles. You'd better get your foot in

your hand or you weren't gonna make it. From those first days until we left the ranch in 1968 or '69, we trotted.

To compound the trotting situation my rifle weighs nearly nine pounds. We always carried a peanut butter sandwich and in the early times some sort of canteen. That damn thing weighed about two pounds for the first mile, but after about ten miles it weighed at least fifty, so we quit that practice. We'd swig a big mouth full of water as we left the vehicle and hope we didn't need any more before we got back late that afternoon.

Sometimes we made it, and many times we thought we were going to die of thirst before we made it back. We'd stuff a small wad of toilet paper in our back pocket (which

Rawls mesa

Not Enough Bullets

Holguin Headquarters—Mule Deer
MEK and Bill Kuykendall, far right

Rawls Ranch scenery

believe it or not was good for two purposes), check to see how many bullets we had in our pockets, and off we'd go.

I know it's hard to believe but we could trot all day and not break a sweat. We'd trot up to the edge of a big canyon, stop, roll some rocks off in it to see what might jump up, and if nothing moved, trot on over to the next one and repeat the process. The main difficulty we had out there was the really big canyons that cut through the ranch. Many of them were 300 feet deep and you had to cross them. If you didn't, it meant you had to go for miles and miles to try and get around one. We found that very impractical, so we always opted to try and cross them. This meant you had to find a way down to the bottom, and then repeat the process to get back out. Some times it might take an hour or more just to cross one of the damn things, when from the top it only seemed like it was a short distance to the other side.

Running Out of Bullets

I was shooting my .270, as per usual, and so was Weldon Seiders, a fellow my cousin Worth had brought out from Austin. Weldon's family owned the Cash & Carry Grocery stores in Austin. I was about to learn one of my many lessons out there and that was being able to correctly answer the question, "Did you bring enough bullets?" A box of .270s held twenty shells. It usually took five or six rounds to shoot the rifle in before the hunt, so that left fourteen or fifteen bullets. Hell, I said, where I come from, if you can't kill something with fourteen or fifteen bullets you might as well stay home.

The first day out, Worth, Weldon and I hunted the same area. We jumped a little buck right off the bat and shot at it one or two times before it got away, unscathed. We hadn't gone over a mile or two before we repeated the process. This time Worth got a little buck down, so we cleaned it, marked the spot with toilet paper so the cowboys could ride in horseback and pick it up, and moved on. We had found out early on that if you marked one of the high ridges with red tape, you couldn't see it at all, but if you marked some of the Ocotillo bushes with strip of white toilet paper, you could see it blowing in the breeze for a mile. Go figure, but now you know why we carried some extra toilet paper.

Then, we jumped a pretty good bunch of deer way down in the bottom of one of the canyons. We ran over and sat on the edge and started shooting at them until they ran out of sight. We didn't hit a one of them and man was that fun, a new way to hunt and bust some caps at the same time. That year Worth had given me one of those new leather shell holders that fit over your belt. It held twenty shells. It had fifteen when I left home, but now I looked and there were only three left. And, I was out on my first day of a seven-day hunt. Thank goodness Weldon shot the same caliber. He had two more boxes back in camp and loaned me some bullets. Valuable lesson number something: "You never have enough bullets!"

The Big One That Got Away

Several days later, I went back to where we had hunted when I had borrowed the bullets from Weldon. I was easing along the side of a big draw when a hell of a buck got up directly across from me, 100 to 150 yards away. He just came up and started to trot from my right to my left, all the time angling up to go over the ridge. I knelt down, and shaking like a leaf, tapped one at him. He humped up like I had gut shot him, but he never quit trotting. In the desert there was nothing for me to get a rest on so I was shooting off hand. I shot at him five more times but I just couldn't hit him. I started to reload as he went over the ridge, but was unable to get another whack at him before he went out of sight. I was sick. He was a hell of a buck. I worked my way down into the draw and up the other side as quickly as I could, and when I topped out on the ridge line, you could see for fifty miles. I squatted down and started looking for dust to see which way he had run. There was nothing as far as I could see. I was very disappointed. You don't get opportunities like that very often and I had messed up big time not being able to hit him again and bring him down.

The Discovery

Many years later, Worth came in and told me a strange tale. While he was working up in those very same ridges, he came upon a rock ledge that had a small crevice under it and in there he found a skeleton of a buck. Even though the rats and varmints had chewed most of the points away, the old buck had ten or fifteen points and was a hell of a big buck. It was the same one. When I had topped that ridge all those years before, that ole' buck had trotted over the top, eased down until he found that rock ledge where he could hide, and was laying there right below me the whole time. What a pity, but it was a valuable lesson learned and I tried to never let that happen again.

A Change of Venue

No sooner had I gotten to Sul Ross in the fall of 1950, when the Korean War started. In those days, you had to register for the draft at eighteen and I was no exception. My draft board soon notified me that I either had to be in an ROTC outfit or I would be drafted immediately and be sent to a very cold region.

Sul Ross had no ROTC; so the second semester of my freshman year, which was the spring of 1951, I transferred to Southwest Texas State in San Marcos because it had an Air Force ROTC unit. To stay in college, I was obliged to sign a contract with that unit agreeing to enter the Air Force upon graduation. I did all that, and when I graduated I entered flight school in one of the last classes trained to fly B-25s, the class of 55-T.

However, this move to San Marcos in no way hindered my early years at the Rawls.

Mr. Herman Heep of Buda

The first years we always stayed at the Holquin house. Worth and his wild bunch stayed in what was known as the Trapper's Cabin. It was a tin shack somewhere between the Holquin and the headquarters, where the ranch stored cottonseed cake and other stuff for the sheep. Worth's bunch always included Uncle Ike of Dripping Springs, Boon Heep, Jr. and Gerald Montague, both from Buda.

In those early years, Dad got his old friend Herman Heep of Buda to lease the entire ranch for the use of his oil company employees. So Dad and I stayed down at Junie's and helped squire his folks around so they'd have a good time. Herman owned a twin engine Beechcraft airplane and he'd fly back and forth during the season, as time permitted, and land up at the main headquarters where Dad would pick him up. He'd then spend perhaps one night, check on his folks to make sure everything was hunky-dory, and fly back to Austin.

Rawls Ranch

During one of these trips, he asked me to accompany a couple of his managers and make sure they both got a deer. I told him I'd be delighted. Mr. Heep had a Jeep station wagon especially designed for hunting. It was one of the first of its kind I had seen, a box-shaped, 4-door. He had some machine shop in Austin chop the top off while leaving the windshield intact. They then cut out all the doors with nothing but a strap across the openings. The back of the front seat had racks built into it so you could hang your rifles or shot-guns there. There was also a built-in box where you could store more ammo and stuff. I thought it was fancy.

One of the hired hands from Heep's ranch at Buda was there to help. He worked around the camp to keep everything in order but was allowed to hunt when he had time. I noticed with some trepidation that the only gun he brought was an old Winchester .30-.30 carbine. Well, heck, I thought, he'll never kill anything with that little popper out here in the wide open spaces.

The next day he had one of the cowboys bring over a horse for him and off he rode. Well, hunting horseback has about seven things going for it and about nine of them are bad. Anyway, off the fellow went. I knew nothing good would come of it. Just after lunch, he returned and damn if he hadn't killed a little buck. As he rolled the buck off that pony, I noticed he'd been shot right behind the left ear. Damn I thought, *that's a pretty good shot with that little carbine.* But I didn't say anything, knowing durn well it was beginner's luck. A day or two later, he went out again, and sure enough, he came back about the middle of the afternoon with another little buck. As he was unloading him, I took a peek and

damn if he hadn't been shot right behind the right ear. I figured I'd better stay out of that fellow's way, 'cause he could sure as hell work with that little pea-shooter.

Horses and Guns

Hunting horseback sounds like fun but it has many drawbacks and some of them are pretty serious. But I got one of the cowboys to saddle me a pony about the same time and went out on a hunt to see what I could do. Well, to start with, my gun was too heavy to carry in a scabbard. I have tried, but it pulls my saddle off balance all day. You are constantly trying to jerk your saddle up so it stays level and that will drive you crazy. So, I always carried the .270 across my lap.

I always wore my lace-up hunting boots in Central Texas and nothing changed when I went to West Texas. But those hunting boots were too big for the stirrups and I worried that I might get one of my feet stuck in one of them, get bucked off, and get *drug* about four miles through the lovely, West Texas landscape and be history.

One of the few good things about being on horseback is that you can travel over lots of country and you are about eight feet above the ground, allowing you to look over the brush. The down side is the reverse: You jump a good buck and spur your horse forward until you get to where you can shoot; you step or fall out of the saddle trying not to hang a hunting boot in the stirrup; you shoot and your horse turns absolutely wrong-side-out, jerks free and runs off. And there you are about eleventeen miles from the house. In the mean time, you missed the buck. I don't like to hunt horseback.

57

Not Enough Bullets

The Backup Shooter

Despite knowing how much trouble you can get into hunting from a horse, one day I decided go out horseback. While watching a chi-chi bird fly by, my pony jumped a little draw, and jerked me forward and crushed the hell out of my left nut. Man, it nearly killed me. I eased back home on the pony and the following day was unable to get out of bed or walk a single step from all the swelling. By the third day, I was a bit better, hobbling around the camp, when Mr. Heep asked me to squire his managers around on a tour. I told him I thought I could do that "*come morning.*"

Mr. Heep always used hired help from the Driskill Hotel in Austin and this year he had employed a guy named Jack.(Can't remember his last name) He drove the Jeep all the way to West Texas, helped around the camp and would drive the vehicle around the ranch when anyone needed it. So, the next morning, I asked both of the managers if they'd like to make a round that day with me, and they said they'd love to. I whistled up Jack to please get the vehicle all warmed up and we were on our way at the crack of dawn.

Dad and I never left camp until it just started to get light. It was not like it is today, where hunters are dressed up in their finery, stay in some lovely lodge, and are squired to a heated deer stand about 4 a.m. to get ready for the day's festivities.

There was game all around our old camp house. A bunch of deer watered there every night and we'd see them each day when we left. There was no need to pull out until one could barely see. So, that's what we did. Jack was, of course, driving. One of the fellows sat in the right front seat and the other sat in the right rear seat. I was sitting directly behind Jack.

I don't think we'd gone over a mile or two when we made a bit of a swing to the south where the ranch road leveled out a bit. We were on the east side of a big hill covered with greasewood and ocotillo. Being early morning, a bright sun was just playing on the upper slope as we eased by. It was still dark on our left, so all of us were looking up to our right to see if anything was moving up there.

Suddenly, Jack stopped the Jeep, turned off the key and said in a very low voice, "Thar he is!" Well, I fell out immediately and quickly hobbled back behind the vehicle until I was clear of the rear bumper. Now, remember, there were no doors on this hunting Jeep, just open spaces, so when Jack made his statement, both men turned their bodies to face the mountain, both with their guns loaded and pointing out side the Jeep. I looked up high on the slope and couldn't see a damn thing. "He ain't up thar, he's right thar," Jack said, pointing off to our right. I looked where Jack was pointing and sure enough, there was a hell of a buck standing not twenty or thirty steps to the right of the Jeep thinking he was hidden because of the darkness. When he said that, I swung up on that ole' buck and said just loud enough for the two fellows to hear, "Which of you are gonna shoot?"

The moment I uttered those words, both men pulled the triggers on their rifles, which, thank God, were pointed down at the side of the road, and blew dirt and rocks all over every thing. The instant that happened I busted that buck and knocked him down. As I was reaching over to shuck in another shell, I hollered, "Which one of you fellows shot him?" In one heart-beat the man in front flew out of the Jeep running toward the deer, hollering, "I got him, I got him," and friends that was it. Mr. Manager had himself one of the best mule deer bucks ever to come off the Rawls ranch. I looked up at Jack and he was grinning at me and just shaking his head from side to side. He knew exactly what had happened. Just call me a "Back-up Shooter."

The Seventeen-Shot Buck

I know it sounds crazy, but in all the years we spent on the Rawls ranch, I think my record for most shots at one deer was seventeen rounds. On top of that, I think I did it three times. Look, I never said I was perfect, nor have I said I was a fabulous shot, *just quick*. And, I am damn proud of it, so there! Any dumb SOB can shoot just once, but what in the hell is the fun in that? If you can't run out of bullets every now and then you might as well stay home and listen to the Green Hornet on Clear Channel radio station WOAI, number 1200 on your dial.

It was in one of the early years at the ranch, when Cousin Worth and I had loped off what seemed like about a hundred miles into the back country. We had come to one of the deep canyons that needed to be crossed and spent about thirty minutes sliding down the near side and damn near an hour panting and struggling to get out the other. Worth and I usually stayed about two or three hundred yards apart as we'd trot through the country. Then, if anything jumped, one or the other of us would get a whack at it. But, since the only way down was an old deer trail, we got bunched up and stayed that way until we finally staggered up the other side.

Just as we topped out of the canyon, we looked to mutual right, and up came eight or ten doe, yearlings and two or three bucks. One of them was a hell of a good one. Both Worth and I instantly unraveled our smoke-

poles. He shot at one as I tapped at another one I saw had plenty of horns. I don't remember if Worth hit his buck or not—I don't think he did—but mine humped up. That meant I'd shot him pretty far back.

The edge of the canyon was filled with big, tall ocotillo, which extended all over the top. Occasionally they have a little red flower on their outer edges and are a beautiful Chihuahua desert cactus. All of the deer were "crow hopping" down through this stuff like a bunch of grasshoppers. Desert mule deer can do this magnificent hop, jumping like kangaroo, all four legs at once.

Obviously, Worth and I were completely winded from the climb, even more so by the unexpected firefight. What I was doing was trying to break the deer's neck just like I'd been able to do at home. So every time I'd swing up my rifle, I'd pull up high and shoot at his head over the tops of the ocotillo. Well, I missed him every time, very quickly running through my first load of six bullets. As soon as I realized what I had done, I reached in my belt and started pulling out shells one at a time, shooting until he disappeared from view. I am pretty sure I got either one or two more whacks at him.

Too Much Hurry-Up

My adrenalin was kicked into overdrive by then and I did what an experienced hunter should never do. I quickly reloaded another six shells, and took off in a high trot after him. I had not given him any time to freeze-up from my first shot; and had I waited fifteen or twenty minutes I would have found him dead.

I probably trotted three or four hundred yards over the top of this high ocotillo-covered mesa, when I ran right up on top of him lying down. Well, I'm here to tell you, when he got up that time, he was carrying the mail. He was still hopping, but each hop seemed like it covered a hundred yards. Turns out I must be a very slow learner, because I shot at his head again, over and over. I cleared about thirty-five acres of prime ocotillo forest until I ran through that load. I'd had a great opportunity to get him down and flubbed it big time. Why in the hell didn't I just shoot him square in the butt and quit this fancy attempt at breaking his neck? In the third place, how in the hell was I going to do that with him hopping in the air all the time. I was sick.

I was mad as hell at myself for letting him get away a second time. How many times are you given a second chance to correct your mistakes, rarely, or *NEVER!*

I knelt down to get my breath and reloaded a second time, carefully putting six more shells in my gun. I waited a bit and saw Worth about three hundred yards away, trotting up on my right flank. I turned and started trotting the way my buck had gone. We both went about a half-mile until we came to a spot where the country fell below us and you could see for miles. There was no dust popping up anywhere. My buck was gone. At that point, I hand signaled to Worth that I was going to backtrack the way I'd come.

The Feeling
Or a Booger in the Brush

Just about everything that grows in the desert has a thorn on it, tough country and tougher plants. However, there is a plant that is real rubbery that does not have thorns. It grows in clumps covering several square yards to maybe an acre or two. I had noticed a bunch of it in my initial trot but paid no attention to it. I was walking slowly back to where the fight had started and while passing within about thirty yards of one of these patches, I suddenly got goose bumps. It was such a strong feeling that I did something really weird. I stopped and waved until Worth saw me. Then without knowing why, I pointed at the clump of stuff to my right and started toward it. Worth realized something was amiss and started jogging in my direction.

The patch of brush that had attracted my attention was about fifty feet across. As I entered the lower side, I took my .270 off safety. Now, mind you, I hadn't seen a thing, I just an overwhelming feeling that something was in that patch. I waded very, very slowly though the stuff, which was quite thick, careful to look where I was going. I stopped every few feet and scanned the whole area. I had walked about twenty or thirty yards into it and was looking over to my left, still moving, when I actually kicked that son of a gun in the butt. What saved me from getting the hell hooked out of me, was one, he was lying away from me, and two, he was so stiff by now that he had trouble getting up, and three, at that very instant, I snapped off a shot.

I was holding the gun down around my waist and the shot missed his skull by a hair, burning all the skin off between his horns. Thank goodness, the blast blew him away from me just enough to keep me from getting run over. With that explosion, he came flying out of there, still hopping. I shot at his head one more time and missed. He was struggling to get away and I ran through big prickly pear I hadn't seen, knelt down, and shot that son of a bitch square in the butt like I should have done about eleven shots before. The famous "Kuykendall Shot" was invented *that* day, on *that* mountain, at *that* moment. And let me tell you what it will do:

Rawls Ranch

It will make a big West Texas mule deer quit that damn "crow hopping."

Even after the *Kuykendall Shot*, when the ole buck's ass hit the ground, he turned around to get a look at me and I shot him right between the eyes. When he hit the ground both his horns folded. I had shot his skullcap in two. I was so blown away by the whole episode that I had to sit down on the ground. Worth came running up thinking I'd been hurt. I was OK, but I had just experienced the most exciting moment in all of my hunting life, though I'm sure I didn't know it until much later when the dust settled.

Why did I decide there was something in that patch? What had set off all my alarms? Worth and I talked about it all that day and we concluded I had probably smelled him and didn't know it. What other reason is there?

All I know is it took a bunch of shots. I could have used a bigger cartridge belt.

MEK—17 shot mule deer
Rawls Ranch

Not Enough Bullets

Later Years: The New Folks

In the years after Herman Heep quit leasing the ranch for his oil company, it fell to Dad to come up with enough hunters to fill the quota for the upper part. I think there were fifteen hunters and if memory serves me, we were all paying $50 a head. As mentioned Grandpa Rawl's Alazan had always gone to friends of his and none of us ever ventured down into his southern part of the 60,000 acres.

Some hunters stayed at Junie's place, Worth and the wild bunch were still at the Trapper's Cabin and Dad and our bunch moved to Jack Senior's, the ranch headquarters where the landing strip was located.

The Smiths from Houston, Ford and his brother Harvey, stayed in another part of the upper ranch, but I don't remember where their camp was located. By this time, Dr. Raleigh R. Ross and his buddy Dr. H. L. Williams of Austin had joined us; Jim Hairston of Rice's Crossing over near Taylor became my hunting buddy; and there were a few scattered friends from Austin like George McCall, H. T. Hibler, Jack Maroney and whoever else Dad could dig up to join us when we were short of hunters.

In our middle years on the ranch, enough folks had started bringing Jeeps every season

Rawls Ranch Trapper's Cabin
Bill Kuykendall, unknown, Gerald Montague, H.T. Hibler, George McCall,
Jack Maroney, Boone Heep Jr, MEK, Jim Hairston, Ike Kuykendall, Worth Hoskins

Rawls Ranch

that Dad convinced the Rawls to push some new roads over different parts of the ranch. This made it much easier to spread the hunters out and it also meant we didn't have to walk so many miles every day just to see something.

Every morning different groups would "saddle up" their vehicles and head off into the unknown. Occasionally, we'd all agree the night before a hunt that everyone would gather in a certain area of the ranch the next day for a drive hunt. A drive hunt was where we'd drop folks off in a line so they could all start walking through the country or sweeping a canyon. Dad and a few others would become what we called blockers. They'd go down to the end and wait and see what came busting out. We'd use this technique a lot as the season wound down and we were still short a deer or two to fill everyone's tags.

The Early Rat Patrol

One day when we'd been driving until our eyeballs were nearly popping out, we all seemed to converge at a particular high point just about noon. There were four Jeep loads of nine people: Dad, Jim Hairston and I made the lone threesome. Raleigh and H. L. rode in another Jeep, Worth and Boon Heep in the third vehicle and Gerald Montague and Uncle Ike in the last.

We were quite a bundle of tired, dusty, bleary-eyed men armed with every style of rifle, carrying large knives and strung with all nature of bullet-filled bandoleers. If we'd been seen in any town, the officials probably would have alerted the Texas National Guard.

Remember, in the old days we had carried four extra bullets in the watch pocket

The Rat Patrol—Rawls Ranch
Bill Kuykendall, MEK, Dr. H.L. Williams & Jim Hairston

Not Enough Bullets

of our Levis. Then we graduated to a small leather cartridge-holder that held twenty rounds; then Worth had a complete cartridge belt that held twenty-five made for both of us; finally, Worth had a bandoleer belt made which I copied that would hold forty-four cartridges, and man, we were in business. I had learned the hard way that you can't carry too damn many bullets. What if you ran out? We looked like a bunch of Gringos riding with Poncho Villa.

There we were, all scattered around our vehicles, trying to spread peanut butter and jelly on a pile of Mexican white bread we had bought at Maria's Half Price Taco Grocery and Self-Serve Gas Station a week earlier in Marfa, when all of a sudden, about fifteen doe, yearlings and assorted bucks came crow hopping out of the canyon to our right and bounced right by us, only about thirty steps away.

"Shit!" we all hollered and what seemed like four hundred slices of Maria's white bread went flying through the air as nine grown men tried to fight their way into a bunch of battered Jeeps to give chase, some clinging on for dear life. This scene could have served as a pilot for the "Desert Rats" TV series.

By the time we had all gotten semi-mounted, the bunch of deer had made it four or five hundred yards to our left, headed for a big canyon on that side. Guess these animals just liked a change of scenery every once in a while. We threw the Jeeps in high gear and went roaring down through the grease wood, dodging the bigger ocotillos as best we could, and watched as that bunch of deer went flying over the lip of the big canyon ahead of us and out of sight.

Forty or fifty yards from the edge of the canyon we were probably doing thirty-five miles an hour in second gear, but it felt like a hundred. At that point, we all jammed the gear-shift into low, reached up and turned off the key, slid right up to the edge of the big canyon, and fell out in a big cloud of dust.

I was driving for Dad and we were on the far left of the pack. When we baled out, I was on the far left side, with Dad next to me and Jim Hairston next to him, and so on. Running and sliding to the lip of the canyon, I took off my forty-four shot belt. When I sat down to shoot, I laid it across my lap so I could get to the bullets easier when I needed them. And need them I did!

By the time we all got in position, the "covey" of deer were in the bottom of the canyon, two to three hundred yards below us. It was not going to be an easy shoot-um-up.

When I first looked over the edge of the canyon the deer were just scurrying out toward the other side. There were three or four bucks, and as I leaned over and shot, eight other people did the same thing, with Dad a hair's-breadth ahead of me with his shot. I know, because Dad was shooting a .300 Weatherby and when he touched that cannon off about ten yards to my right I flinched.

It seemed like the whole canyon bottom below us turned to dust. The does went one way and the two bucks that survived that first onslaught came staggering out the other side of the dirt, dust and flying rocks caused by all the shots. I remember Dad's shot, because not only did I feel the muzzle blast, but I heard the very distinct sound of a bullet hitting a deer square in the butt. It's a big "ka-whump," unlike any other sound. Not to mention the fact that when Dad shot, that particular buck reared up and fell over backwards. I thought, *Oh shit, Dad's "Kuykendall'd" him... forget about eating those hams.*

Forgetting about Dad's buck, I quickly ran through the balance of my load whacking at the bigger of the two bucks that had been hit but were still running. I know, you are supposed to take your time and shoot, but not when you are in "hurry-up mode" trying to shoot faster than everyone else.

I started single loading as soon as I'd run through the first batch of shells. By the time the bigger of the two bucks had staggered over the far ridge, I'd probably shot another half-dozen rounds. The last few shots were more lobs than anything, because by the time the wounded buck cleared the other side of the hill and went out of sight, the distance was seven or eight hundred yards—almost half a mile. You'd shoot just to see where the dust splatter was, then correct and shoot again. After the shooting stopped, those who were interested started to filter their way off the ridge to see what Dad had killed.

Raleigh hollered at me and said he thought he was the one who had wounded the bigger buck and did I want to go with him to look for it. I said I'd be happy to, mounted his ole' Jeep and off we went.

We had to go up the canyon about a half-mile to get down and across the other side. Since that side was not as steep as the one we were on, we were able to ease up and crest over the ridge for a look-see.

The other side of the canyon was not as dramatic as where we had been. The country smoothed out a lot and immediately became light greasewood as far as you could see. Except for a small, shallow, brush-filled draw about two hundred yards below us, running from our right to our left, there was no cover whatsoever. Raleigh and I looked at one another and nodded. That ole' buck had to be down in that little draw cause there wasn't any brush anywhere else big enough to cover your hat.

I motioned to Raleigh to stay up along the side the hill, and I'd fall off in that draw and commence to stomp my way down it to see what might come out. Once I got down in it, the brush was taller than my head, so I couldn't see anything. I hadn't pushed my way through that stuff more than seventy-five yards when I heard an animal bust out ahead of me. Then there were two quick shots from Raleigh's Model 21 .30-06 Remington pump. I crawled out of the cut I was in and sure enough, Mr. Buck had run out on his side and was down. We gutted and loaded him in the Jeep and headed back to the others.

A Perfect Kuykendall Shot

Our sojourn had probably taken about an hour. Jim, Dad, and several others stood clustered around Dad's buck. We drove right up to them and Dad motioned for us to get out, that there was something he wanted to show us. Now Dr. Raleigh R. Ross was one of the most renowned surgeons in all of Texas. So Dad, with a smirk on his face said, "Doctor, see if you can tell where I hit him."

Well, Raleigh, eased out of his Jeep, put on his gold-rimmed bifocals like he was getting ready to go into surgery and started to examine the deer. Dad hadn't gutted the buck yet, so we rolled him over and there was no bullet-hole anywhere. Even his bung-hole, which as best Raleigh could ascertain, had not been disturbed by the entry of a .300 caliber bullet from the field piece Dad was shooting. His inspection did, however, reveal that both his testicles and most of his penis were no where to be found. Then, the good doctor straightened up, dusted himself off, folded his glasses, stuck them back in his pocket, and said, "Well, I'll tell you one damn thing,

Not Enough Bullets

if he'd a shot my balls off with that .300 Weatherby, I'd be dead too." And with that, we all broke into to howls of laughter.

Dad had shot at that buck just as he bottomed out. The bullet had, indeed, gone down between his hind legs and had blown everything off and killed that son of a gun dead as a hammer.

Flying to Rawls

In 1956, Dad and Lat Maxcy of Florida bought a 139-section ranch in the state of Coahuila, Mexico, just over the mountains from the village of Muzquiz. He also purchased a Cessna 172 from Bobby Ragsdale in Austin to get back and forth. When I got out of the Air Force in 1957, I went down there to join him as the designated ranch pilot.

We had built an airstrip on our ranch at Kyle, so when the mule deer season was getting ready to start, we flew up to the Kyle ranch from Muzquiz. Dad and I spent the night there and got all our gear together and took off the next morning for the Rawls ranch. Everyone else in our bunch had already gone out, towing their Jeeps and other gear, and they were awaiting our arrival.

The morning of our departure from the Kyle ranch, the weather was horrible. A cold front was just approaching so we had a low overcast and lots of scud. Being the fearless aviators we were, we took off and headed west.

Now a Cessna 172 is not the best instrument airplane in the sky, number one, and number two, I had been flying it for a year in the mountains of northern Mexico. In that part of the world there was a cardinal rule: One does not fly into clouds. The English translation is this: "In Mexico, the clouds are full of rocks!"

So, after a year down there, I had completely forsaken my excellent instrument training and had opted for a policy of "if you can see, you can go." Well, heck, we could see, almost.

The Kyle airstrip elevation is about 950 feet above sea level. The country we were heading into quickly rose to more than 2,000 feet in the Sonora/Ozona area and 3,000-4,000 feet in the mountains of West Texas.

We headed out and I immediately found U.S. Highway 290 about Fredericksburg and lined up with it as my roadmap. We had been flying through scud all along which would limit visibility for a bit then clear up a tad. It was not perfect, but we knew, or figured, that since it seldom rains in West Texas, the weather had to get better the farther west we flew.

Sure enough, as we passed over Junction, the ceiling lifted a wee bit and we winged on toward Sonora. We were flying at about 500 feet the whole way, so we didn't have a lot of maneuvering room. As we approached Sonora, the ceiling began to lower rapidly. On the way to Ozona, the clouds got lower still. Actually, we were flying at the same altitude, the elevation of the terrain below was rising rapidly under us and we didn't realize it.

The Windmill

By now, the hills on either side of the airplane were higher that we were and I was practically having to dodge eighteen wheelers on the highway. About that time Dad said, "Don't you think we're flying a bit low?" I answered, "Why do you think that?" He said, "'Cause, I just saw the tail on that windmill we passed and it said, AERMOTOR, Chicago, Ill. written on it!" Oh!

We then went whizzing around the next curve of the highway at about 130 miles an hour and flew straight into a cloud bank. I mean one minute you can see a few feet in front of you and the next instant you couldn't see the prop turning over on the front of the airplane.

Dad hollered, "Turn around!" Without hesitation, I jerked that little airship straight up on its tail. There was no turning around. I had already violated about seventeen rules of flying, and turning around in a narrow canyon with rocks about four feet either side of me suddenly did not seem like an option.

I hung it on the prop, knowing any second we might hit one of the canyon walls and held my breath for what seemed like an eternity. I kept the nose straight up until my airspeed bled off down to about 80 mph, which was my climbing speed. By that time, I finally took a breath, knowing we had cleared all the canyon rims.

We couldn't see our wing tips it was so thick. I kept my climbing airspeed at 80 mph, heading west toward Fort. Stockton. We didn't break out in the clear until we passed 8,000 feet. My shirt was wet through and through. About Bakersfield, the overcast broke just like you cut it with a knife, and we flew into the clear. We landed in Fort Stockton, not because we needed fuel, but because we needed to go to the bathroom and wash our faces to get the sweat off. After we got our breathing under control, we took off again and flew to the Rawls headquarters, where someone picked us up. Some start for a relaxing hunt, huh?

Smoke in the Air

Several days later, Dad said he wanted to make a round and asked if I would go with him. Someone was using our Jeep that day, so we borrowed the ranch pickup. Dad had

missed a buck or two and at nearly sixty-eight was feeling a bit down in the dumps, perhaps thinking he was slipping a peg or two.

It was late when we got cranked up, probably 10:30 A.M. and, as is typical in early December in West Texas, probably around 80 degrees. I figured it would be a waste of time to go out, but *oh, well*. Dad wanted to drive and off we went. I think he mainly wanted me to go with him so I could open the damn gates. We had gone through two or three gates already and were sailing along about thirty mph down a relatively level stretch of road across the mesa, when I looked out to my right and said, "Whoa, there he is!"

Just out to my right, not fifty steps, was a pretty good buck. We had surprised him by coming up so quickly. He tried to hunker down in the greasewood to hide, but Dad jammed the truck into third gear, turned the key off and slid to a stop, all in one motion.

As soon as the truck quit moving, Dad baled out and laid his .300 across the hood of the truck. As he was doing that, I opened the passenger's side door and turned to face the buck. I snapped the safety off and got in my bowed up tomcat stance to be ready. At that instant Mr. Buck figured he'd better get the hell out of there and lunged forward. One ten thousandth of a second later, Dad touched off his cannon. Well, nothing happened cause Dad had apparently missed. One second later, he hollered, "Gawd-damn, aren't you gonna shoot?" And before he got the word "shoot" out of his mouth, I jerked my rifle up and let 'er fly.

Man, you have never seen so much white smoke in your life! I shot both his horns off and *ass-over-tea-kettle* he went in a big cloud of volcanic dust, rocks and gravel. You'd of thought I'd shot through a ten-pound sack of Aunt Jemima Flour. As I reached over the top of my gun to rack in another shell, I glanced up and saw little white things floating downward in the air. Those were all that was left of both of his horns. I had shot his horns clean off, killing that son of a gun dead as a doornail.

Dad and I went up to see the damage and field dress the deer. As we rolled him over, we noticed a clean cut about an inch deep right across the back of his butt, just enough to barely cut the skin and blow all the hair off. That is where Dad's bullet hit had hit him. When the buck bolted, Dad hadn't swung with him. Such is the life of a hunter.

My Bullets

I am no authority on ballistics, but a lot of good hunters are. While the pre-war .270 Winchester is one of the best rifles ever produced by the company, a minor problem with the caliber was a lack of bullet-weight variety. I think the .270 only comes in two bullet weights, 130 and 150 grains. The .30-06 caliber, on the other hand, is offered in bullets weights ranging from 180 to 220 grains of lead. If one is hunting deer or similar- size animals, the smaller weights are adequate, but if you wanted to shoot an elk or a bear, it might be best to use a heavier bullet.

Somewhere in the course of things, I ran across a 130-grain cartridge that had a bronze tip. What I liked about it was two fold: One, the point didn't get messed up in my hunting belt causing it to become inaccurate, and two, when it entered the cavity of an animal, the damn thing exploded. Let me explain: The bronze tip was so hard that as the bullet penetrated the body of an animal, the still-intact tip would be driven backward into the case of the bullet, causing it to shatter. When it shattered or blew-up, little pieces

of the shell casing would fly all through the body, just like shrapnel from a small hand-grenade. So, if I shot a deer too far back and missed his vitals, the bronze-tipped bullet usually would kill him anyway. Unless, of course, I jumped him too quickly and ran the sucker off.

In the early days Dad bought most of our hunting stuff from the Petmecky sporting goods store at 4th and Congress Avenue in Austin. They had been there forever and were well known. Sometimes he'd take me around the corner on Brazos and we'd visit with old J. F. Buster Kruse. Buster had a little one-man gun shop and occasionally Dad would buy something from him.

As the years progressed I started buying all my stuff from the McBride family, who own a sporting goods store at 29th and North Lamar in Austin. Before any of our trips I'd call in and have some member of that fine family find me about four boxes of my bronze-point bullets and put them aside for me. Jack, the father, and then later, Joe, would always take good care of me. Their store is probably the best in all of Texas and the Southwest. A finer bunch of folks do not exist than the McBride family.

Rawls Ranch

Last Years at Rawls

In the later years at the Rawls Ranch, which would have been about 1966-1968, we kept seeing more and more little bucks. Turns out the Rawls needed money just like everybody else and had been double-teaming the country. That means that when we left, the Rawls brought a new group of hunters in behind us. They were killing all the little fours and sixes we had left. So, when we got out there in those last years thinking we'd see some better bucks that would now be two- and three-year-olds, all we saw were spikes and four-pointers.

Just about the time we figured it out and started to complain a bit, Junie upped the lease on us from $50 to $80 per person. How dare he? So, at the end of the 1968 season, we quit the Rawls ranch in a huff over everything. We had been out there eighteen years.

I laugh when I think back on it now. In the later years, Texas turned into the premier hunting state in the nation (outside of Alaska). That West Texas mule deer lease today would cost $1,500 to $2,500 a gun. Jack Bowman's ranch will cost a cool $10,000 or better, per man, *AND* you will be limited to one buck only. How fortunate we were to be able to hunt in the heyday of Texas hunting.

Jack McBride
McBride's Store

69

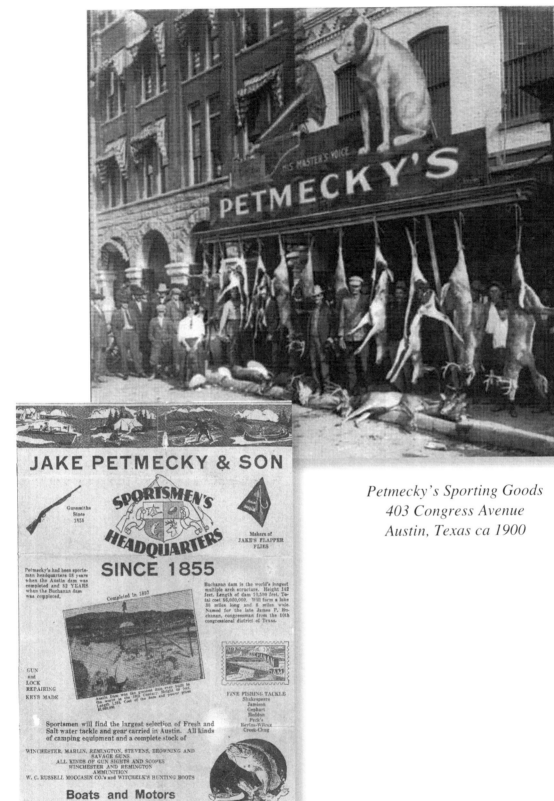

Petmecky's Sporting Goods
403 Congress Avenue
Austin, Texas ca 1900

The Other Story, Part II

Now back to the opening story in this book. I scrambled out of that draw and shot at that mule deer, and knew I'd shot underneath him. So, for him to rear up, fall over backwards and jam his horns in the ground came as about as much a shock to me, as I'm sure, it was to him. I always reload and as I approached that buck, the hair was standing up on the back of my neck.

When I make the comment that I get bowed up like a tomcat getting ready to fight, I think most of you know what I mean. You've seen an ole' tom edging up toward another cat, all bowed up, with his hair sticking ever-which-way. Well, that was always the way I approached any animal that was down. You never know what is gonna blow-up in your face and try to eat'cha. I know, deer don't eat people, but try and tell that to my nervous system.

As I eased up on that old buck I was so keyed up that if you'd hollered at me, I swear my feet would have run off at least a hundred yards. I wouldn't have wanted to go with them, mind you, but they would have carried the rest of my body with them.

The buck was about a hundred yards away and basically lying on his back with his feet in the air. When I got closer, which took a bit of time, I realized that sucker was dead as a mackerel. As I rolled him around to see where I'd hit him, I noticed a little tiny bullet hole under his rib-cage where the bullet had just clipped him as it passed underneath his body. The hole was at the bottom of the ribs where they stop and the diaphragm that separates the heart, lungs and liver from the area where the stomach or guts are located. If you poke your finger there, you will find a soft spot in that location.

My bronze-pointed bullet had just barely sliced under his hide but as it passed over that soft spot, the damn thing exploded and blew little jagged pieces of metal back up into his main cavity. That killed him dead. He never knew what hit him. But hold on, the story "ain't" over yet.

I cleaned him and went to get some help in hauling him back to camp. We hung him up in the shed behind the camp to cool and dry out. All our deer had to hang for long periods, because in those days we didn't cut them up until we got home. Incidentally, desert mule deer seem to have a worm or larvae that stay in their throat or nose. When you hang one up by his head, those damn things will drain back into his cavity and he'll spoil. So Dad and I got in the habit of rolling a buck over on his back and cutting him up the throat from his cavity all the way past his tongue to his lower jaw bone, removing his windpipe, tongue and all. We then hung him up, and stuck a stick between his ribs to spread them out so he'd dry out better.

Not Enough Bullets

Well, I did all this, but about two days later, I happened to step behind the shed to check on everything and noticed a hell of a stink. Something was rotten. We had a bunch of deer hanging up by then and as I walked along them trying to figure out where the smell was coming from, I came to my deer. And man, something stunk. I got some help and untied him and pulled him out where I could check him over. As I grabbed one of his forelegs, I think it was the left one, instead of being stiff like it should have been by then, the durn thing was completely loose. I took out my knife and started cutting the foreleg loose when all of a sudden I cut into some putrid stuff and God, it was awful!

Turns out when that damn bullet exploded, not only did it blow up into the cavity, it had sent fragments flying sideways, basically blowing his left foreleg out of its socket. Further compounding the situation, there was food stuff, grasses, weeds, and other matter in that area. Now how in the hell that bullet had done all that damage is beyond my pay grade of understanding, but it had. That sucker was rotting from that stuff and if I had not found it that day, the whole deer would have spoiled. I'm here to tell you, that .270 caliber 130-grain, bronze-pointed cartridge is one hell of a bullet.

Always Take the Shot

Raleigh Ross and I were talking about shooting one day and he re-emphasized the need to get your bullet in the animal. Don't worry about where, just do the best you can with your shot. But above everything else, get a bullet in him; you can work out the details later. Those of you whose eyebrows are starting to lift and whose sneer is starting to appear should relax. I am talking

about big cavity animals of North America, but that absolutely does not include any type of bear.

Everyone in America knows who the Harlem Globe Trotters are. You can have the finest dribbler in the world, an individual unstoppable on the basketball court who can dribble between his legs and yours, but there is a profound mathematical fact that does not require a degree from MIT to understand: If that basketball player DOES NOT shoot at the basket, HE IS NOT GOING TO MAKE ANY POINTS.

Now remember, my hunting days were long ago, mainly on large private ranches. When the opportunity arose to shoot, if I didn't take it when I could, I usually regretted it. I can't tell you how many good deer I have passed up in the first part of a hunt, never to see anything again after that. A bunch!

I have shot at deer when everyone was finished; I have shot at them a mile off and at four feet; I have shot at them in the bottom of big canyons and across larger ones; I have shot at them in timber and brush so damn thick you couldn't drive a Bradley tank through it. There is no situation in the wilds of Texas that I haven't shot in, over or through. Always take the shot. If you don't shoot, you're outcome is guaranteed.

Unexpected Visitors

There is a distinct difference in hunting in the Texas Hill Country, the brush country of South Texas, and the desert of deep West Texas. But one or two things do remain constant. Any time you are gutting a deer and the day is cold, calm and crisp, any smell generated seems to stay close to the ground. On days like that, you want to be damn sure you

The Opening Story, Part II

keep your rifle where you can get your hands on it because every now and then, when you least expect it you are going to have a visitor.

Say you have just shot your deer. You are sitting down somewhere close by to get your breath and let the adrenalin bleed off. You take off your jacket to keep from getting any blood on it, and roll up your sleeves for the same reason. You finally take a big breath, stand up, and figure where you're gonna drag him to so you can gut him. You lay your rifle on your jacket, or if you are me, you always lean it in the nearest bush, barrel up, to keep it out of the dirt. You push and pull until you get the ole' buck where and how you want him. If it's my deer, he's on his back. You cut into him and the steam and hot smell of blood comes rolling out of him. You are working up a sweat trying to get him open and not cut

a big hole in his guts, when you hear a little tiny sound and look up. And, right there, not ten feet from you, is a hell of a big buck and he is all fuzzed up . He has either been traveling with the buck you killed, or perhaps just following the same doe your buck was following. Doesn't matter! He has gotten a big whiff and he's coming to see what it is and, Oh, he is ready to fight.

You look at him, he looks at you, and then you glance over to where your rifle is. Guess what? It's just out of reach! That's because in all your *doings* to get ready to gut your deer, you forgot lesson *Number Something*: Keep your rifle where you can get to it in a hurry. I can't tell you how many times that's happened to me, but after a time or two it will damn sure help you change your habits when it comes to field dressing game.

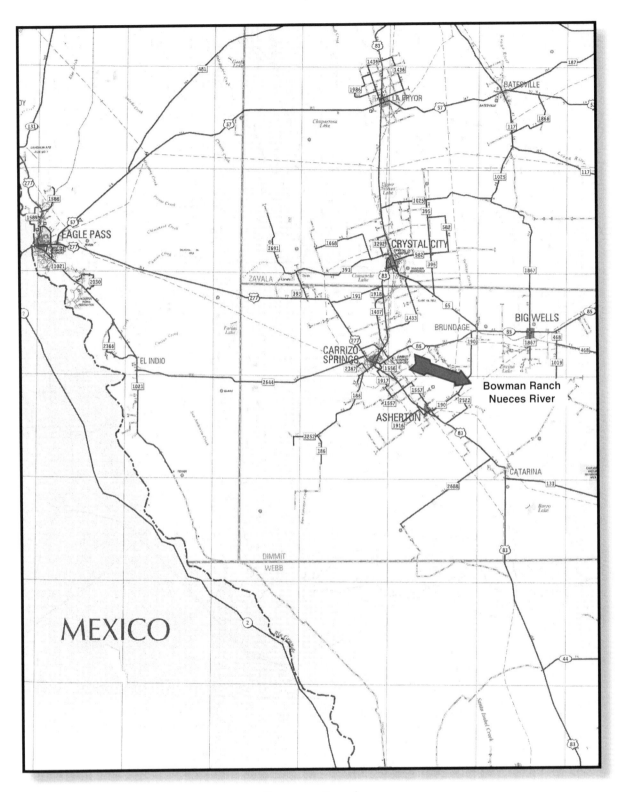

Bowman Ranch

The Jack Bowman Ranch

The Bowman's are an old Austin family. A long avenue in the Tarrytown neighborhood is named after them. Like Niles Graham, and the Reed family, the Bowman's were instrumental in some of the earliest development of old Enfield.

I never knew the older Mrs. Bowman, who was the mother of Bob Bowman of Austin and Jack Bowman of San Antonio. Well, turns out this woman was involved in a terrible car wreck, and as Dr. Raleigh R. Ross explained it to us, "Her head was cut off in the wreck and I sewed it back on and made it work."

Well, Jack Bowman was so thankful for Raleigh's work that he blurted out, "Why don't you come down to South Texas and hunt on my ranch?" Raleigh said, "Absolutely, if I can make a father/son hunt out of it and invite one or two others." Jack said, "Sure, bring them on," or words to that effect.

The doctor called me in the middle of the night to see if Dad and I wanted to go on the hunt. "You bet your life," I answered, adding that I was getting out of bed that instant and getting my stuff together.

The Bowman's ranch is just south of Brundage and Big Wells, in Dimmit County, better known in Texas as Big Buck Country. The ranch covers thousands of acres in many different pastures. The agreement with Raleigh was that he would have the run of a 10,000 acre pasture south of Big Wells that fronted on the Nueces River. Furthermore, Raleigh could choose when he wanted to hunt. He chose after Christmas, which threw our hunt over the time when the big South Texas bucks start the first part of their "rut" or mating season.

Now, we were still hunting at the Rawls Ranch every season. That hunt usually fell over the Thanksgiving weekend. In those days, the Rawls hunt might only be for only three or four days, since that was way before the state began allowing longer hunts in the Trans-Pecos. It was no problem for us to hunt South Texas also.

Remember, I said earlier, that there are "some-time hunters," "maybe hunters," "week-end hunters," and then there was us. To say the least, we were hardcore hunters who loved the out-of-doors. Most of us were very well seasoned long before we ever got to West Texas. It didn't matter what happened, my bunch just got better and better at hunting. It could rain on us, blow on us, dust on us; we could run out of food, run out of water, have four flats on a Jeep, or kill a buck down in a mile-deep canyon—it just didn't matter. We'd *gut-up* and get with the program.

Occasionally, we'd have to deal with men who just thought they wanted to hunt. I remember some men from Austin who came out to the Rawls in those early years. After three or four days of dust, dirt, grime, thirst, and maybe at least one good dose of cheap whiskey, they eased out of the camp, threw their bags in their vehicles, and drove 450 miles back to Austin, never to discuss the experience again.

I mention this because those of us who were fortunate enough to get to hunt on the Bowman ranch were not novices. There was Raleigh and his son, Trip, Dr. Abner Ross, Raleigh's older brother from Lockhart and his son Bubba, and then there was Dad and I. A pretty damn good bunch of hunters. In fact, we thought we were so good that on the back of our mutual hunting trailer was painted the words: "Professional Hunters Association of America," with all our hunts listed.

When Jack explained apologetically that the 10,000-acre pasture on the Nueces was real brushy, had only a crappy old cabin where we could camp and that his cowboys said there weren't many good bucks over there, we jumped at it.

My wife, Karen and I were living in Austin at this time, on the corner of Ridgewood Road and Gentry. Dad and Alice were back at the Kyle ranch. So, on the day after Christmas, I threw all my stuff in my vehicle, went out and met Dad at the ranch, hooked up our Jeep, and took off. We met Raleigh in San Marcos and "caravanned" the rest of the way.

We all went by the Bowman headquarters and picked up the keys to the ranch gate from Jack. Then we gassed up in Big Wells, got a couple more things at the little store there and drove on down to the pasture. We unlocked the gate, went in, locked it behind us and made our way down toward the Nueces River until we came to a little knoll on which sat our "home away from home." It looked like this little wood-framed shack

hadn't been inhabited (I started to say lived in) in a hundred years. It had a porch of sorts and an old rock fireplace and chimney, but no windows. The whole thing leaned about 22.5 degrees that-a-way. Still, we were tickled to have something with a roof and walls. We unloaded our gear and cleaned up the old place as best we could. I think it had three or four rooms. Dad had brought one of the hired hands, so while he was chopping wood for the fireplace, we moved all our hunting paraphernalia inside.

Now chainsaws hadn't been invented yet, but Dad's chainsaw snoring had, along with Bubba Ross's. We put the two of them in one room and the rest of us got another one. We used an old door we found for a table and we were ready. Pretty soon, we had the old place looking like a castle, well, kinda.

The Executive Drive-By

We spent the first night and the following morning making a round or two and killed a buck or two. We were back at the cabin, when who should drive up to check on us, but the man himself, Mr. Jack Bowman. Just came over to be sure we'd made it all right and were set up, he said.

Now don't ask me why some rich men put up with "hanger-oners" but Jack seemed to thrive in that environment. He showed up in his fancy King Ranch hunting vehicle and had two fellows from San Antonio with him. I think one was a lawyer and the other might have been a CPA.

Now, not to digress, but in the Southwest there are occasions when one might call another a "good son of a bitch," or maybe someone would comment that a particular fellow was a "hunting son of a bitch" or an endearing statement like that. But, never in your whole born days will you ever hear anyone say, "You know, that fellow is a good chicken-shit."

Well, I don't remember about the CPA, but the lawyer came prancing in "our castle" and started tossing around phrases like, "pretty seedy bunch" or "look at their worthless crap,"and things like that. All the while Jack is explaining the rules of the hunt to Raleigh. Then, the lawyer fellow eases over to our magnificent dinner table where there are several bottles of Cutty Sark and Johnny Walker Red Label. He picks up one in each hand, and says real loud so Jack will hear him, "Looks like these bastards stole some of your whiskey, Jack," and commences to haul a couple of the bottles out to Jack's car. I saw what he had done and start to stand up when I got a high-sign from Dad to sit back down. I was still seething over the actions of this sorry chicken-shit when I realized why Dad had kept me in check; better to lose a couple bottles of whiskey than to get kicked off a fabulous 10,000 acre hunting ranch after only twenty-four hours.

All the time ole' Jack is just humming along telling Raleigh this and that about the ranch and paying the shit-head lawyer from San Antonio "no never mind,"

The Great Dimmit County Fire

The following day we made an early round which I don't remember, but I do remember what happened right after lunch. Raleigh said, "Let's go make another round while your dad and Dr. Abner are taking a nap." We jumped in my Jeep and off we went. We went two or three miles and had driven down through a bunch of sacahuista (a saw-grass type plant) along the river when I turned the Jeep back toward our camp. We

were astounded to see a massive column of black smoke rising hundreds of feet in the air.

We ran along the road until we could get a better look and when we broke out where we could see up toward the cabin, all we saw were flames and smoke billowing up from it. Everything seemed to be on fire.

A lot of things scared us about that fire. One, Dad and Dr. Abner had been asleep in there when we left; and two, all of our trucks and cars were parked against the building. So, you can imagine our fear as we raced along the rough ranch trail, throwing stuff out of the Jeep as we tore along.

As we rounded the last curve and ran up the hill to the cabin, we were relieved to see Dad and Dr. Abner standing outside. All the cars had been pulled away from the flames and there was gear scattered all over the hill.

The weather was cool and we had kept the fireplace going the entire time we were there. Dad had one of his famous stew pots in the edge of it cooking the whole time. What we didn't know was that the fireplace hearth had a crack in it. As the fire got hotter some coals had fallen down in that crack and overnight had started a smoldering fire in one of the floor joists underneath the old cabin. As the next day wore on, it got hotter and hotter until right after lunch, the beam burst into flames.

The hired hand we had working there saved Dad and Dr. Abner's lives. He kept hearing a crackling sound and not knowing what it was, went outside and knelt down to look under the building. He later said all he saw were flames. The whole under side of the building was on fire. What is even more amazing was that when he ran inside to wake up Dad, neither of them knew that Dr. Abner was asleep in the other room. They didn't notice Dr. Abner, all bundled up in his bed,

Not Enough Bullets

until they started dragging and throwing everything out of the building.

By the time we got there, which was not long after the fire started, they had managed to move all the cars and throw everything out far enough so stuff wouldn't burn. Unbelievably, all we was lost was a 90-cent camp stool and one Coleman lantern. Well, the cabin was gone. I mean, there wasn't anything left but a pile of twisted roofing tin laying on the ground, and one ole' chimney sticking up in the air.

"Well, what to do?" After two minutes of being relieved that no one was dead and all our stuff has been saved by the quick actions of two old men and one very scared ranch hand, Raleigh commenced to walk in large circles, all the time, muttering, "Oh me, oh me, oh me, what shall we do now?"

Finally after about fifteen minutes of that, he said, "Y'all come over here. OK, here's the deal. We either go over to the main headquarters and fess-up to what we have done and take our medicine or go home the back way and never talk to that no-good son of a bitch again!" I swear that's exactly what he said.

So, we loaded everything up and went all the way over to the main headquarters about 40 miles away, to fess up.

Fess Up Time

It was late afternoon by the time we got to the headquarters where Jack lived, a big beautiful ranch home with yard, gardens, barns, corral, and other amenities, a paradise in the brush country.

Great Dimmit Co. Fire—Bowman Ranch
Worker, Bill Kuykendall, Bubba Ross, Dr. Abner Ross, Dr. Raleigh R. Ross

The Jack Bowman Ranch

We drove into the courtyard area looking like a bunch of smoke and dust covered gypsies. As we parked and got out, we could see Jack over in a big oat patch adjacent to the house, squiring some pilgrim around in his fancy King Ranch hunting car. Grazing out in the middle of that patch was one of the biggest South Texas bucks I had ever seen. We stood there with our mouths open while Jack drove right up to that ole' buck, positioned the car so the pilgrim could shoot, and then BLAM. The ole' buck would trot off a little ways and Jack and his guest would repeat the process. I swear he did that three times before the buck finally got tired of being disturbed and trotted over, jumped the fence and disappeared into the thick brush beyond. I had never seen anything like it in my life. I could have killed that ole' buck from the parking lot.

Then Jack turned the vehicle and drove over through the cattleguard to where we were all sheepishly standing, looking down at our boots, all the while moving the gravel around with our toes. Then Jack stopped the fancy vehicle and said, "Howdy, Doctor, what brings you fellows over here? Ya'll didn't burn my house down, did you?"

"Well kinda," answered Raleigh.

Then Jack let out a howl of laughter. "Shit, Raleigh, you could've seen the Gawd-damn smoke from Laredo," he said, and reached in his pocket and pulled out a set of keys. "Here, take these, they are to the gate across the road from the pasture where you're hunting. There's a good house over there with running water and everything. You will like it. Been meaning to burn that damn ole' shack down for years. You boys saved me the trouble."

Raleigh stuck the keys in his pocket and we all started to mount up when Jack hollered,

"And Doctor... Yeah! — Don't burn THAT sum-bitch down."

A Minor Drinking Problem

And then there was Red Whatshisface. We hadn't been situated in our new abode more than a day or two, hunting our butts off every day, when about dark-thirty one evening, up drives the twin brother to Ichabod Crane in a cowboy suit. He was sandy haired, hence his nick-name, about six feet tall, skinny as a rail, had on his cowboy boots and an ole' western straw hat that looked like he'd run over it in his pickup at least once a day. Raleigh had told us about this fellow. He was supposedly Jack's man in charge of hunting and hunters on the whole ranch and he'd come by to "check on us." What he really came by for was our whiskey. That son of a gun could drink a quart of sort-of-good whiskey at a setting. He came stomping in, sat down around our little table and commenced to do just that.

Well, hell, we were *invitees*. So what did we do? We stayed up half the night pouring that son of a bitch drinks. About 2:30 a.m. he finally staggered out of the house for the forty-mile drive back to the ranch headquarters. We were dead tired for three days, not from drinking, mind you, but just from having to put up with ole' Ichabod.

And, the second year we hunted the ranch, damn if he didn't do it again. Now, we had been given the hunting rights for four years; and we hunted each year for three, missed a year and then hunted the last year. I can't remember why we skipped a year.

We always hunted the day after Christmas until sundown on December 31. So, on the third year, as we were getting ready to leave Austin and go down to the ranch, Raleigh called me and asked if I was going to the grocery store. I replied that I was and he asked me to do him a favor and please pick up a pint bottle of Everclear. Now, I didn't know what Everclear was. Turns out it is 190-proof alcohol. I don't have a clue what it is used for, but I bought a pint.

The Cure

We got all situated at the ranch and had hunted two or three days, when sure enough, who should show up but ole' dingbat himself. We were worn out from a good day's hunt and were not very happy to see our old buddy. He came strutting in the house, grabbed a bottle of whiskey, poured himself a big stiff drink and flopped down at the table to make a night of it at our expense.

By 9 or 10 p.m., ole' Red had consumed three or four stout drinks and was getting rubber-legged as hell when he hollered and said he wanted another drink. Raleigh nodded at me and I got up to do the honors. When I got in the kitchen, I poured out his drink, which was in a big waterglass, filled it back up with ice and then, unscrewed the cap on the Everclear and filled his glass to the top. Hauled that sucker back in the other room and ole' Red grabbed it and damn near chugga-lugged the whole thing right then and there.

In about three-and-a-half minutes, he got up to take a leak and fell flat on his butt. We all hollered, "Durn, Red, you want to go home now?" He mumbled something we couldn't understand, so we got him up, and

with one of us on either side to steady him, hauled his butt out to his pickup. By then, Raleigh had the truck turned around and pointed at the highway with the engine running and the lights on. We loaded that son of a gun up and hollered, "Adios, Red," and muttered, "You damn idiot," and pointed toward the highway.

When ole' Red took off, he kinda reminded us of a bucking horse coming out of the chute—snorting, farting, stumbling, and falling all at once. He had the engine revved to about a million rpm's. The old pickup was, of course, standard shift. So, when he finally let the clutch out, he slung dirt and gravel about fifty yards by us, and took off in a big cloud of dust without the usual "Hi-Yo Silver, Away!"

Our camp house was about a mile from the highway. A barbed wire fence ran right down the side of the ranch road. We hadn't quite made it into the house when we heard a big screech of wire-to-metal followed by a big thump or two. The next morning when we left to go that way to cross over to the other pasture, we drove by at least three big gashes in the fence where the posts had been sheared off and in one spot the wire was completely torn loose. How in the hell he'd been able to stop and unlock the front gate, much less go through it, remains a mystery to this day

We heard later that Mr. Whatshisface was slightly under the weather and would no longer be visiting any hunters for the remainder of that season.

BOWMAN RANCH, PART II
Raleigh's Big Buck

The first two years we hunted on the Bowman Ranch, we killed two bucks a piece. When Jack finally figured out we weren't the city slickers he usually had, he told us from then on to only kill one buck each for fear we'd kill everything from there to Carrizo Springs, Texas.

We killed some hellacious good bucks in those years. We made it a rule not to shoot anything under ten points and never did. Didn't kill any Boone and Crockett bucks, but we got close.

One morning we were hunting in the Jeep with the top off and the windshield down. Dad was driving. Raleigh was in the right front seat and I was standing up in the back holding on to the rollbar. It was right at daybreak, cold, with a dense fog. We had just made a 90-degree turn to the left down a long *sendero*, when a buck crawled under the fence about thirty steps in front of us and started to stand up to his full height. (Deer in South Texas crawl under the fences, don't jump them.) By the time he stood straight up, Dad had the Jeep stopped and the engine killed. Raleigh took a deep breath and BOOM, that deer was down. The whole thing happened within a two or three count. I mean see him, stop the Jeep, think and shoot. When he hit the ground and rolled over on his side, his horns were sticking up about two feet. I am here to tell you, he was a big buck. He had fourteen points, sixteen-inch brow tines and must have had a twenty-four to twenty-five inch spread. Unfortunately, we don't have a single picture from those days. You'll just have to take my word for it.

Some Fancy Rattling

One morning when it was still dark, Raleigh and I were down in the same area of the Bowman Ranch where he had killed his big buck. He wanted to do some "rattling," so he had his rattling horns and I had mine. We were at the same spot where the previous year he had killed that fourteen-pointer. Just short of the 90-degree turn in the *sendero* was a big mesquite tree that held up a crude deer stand.. I eased to a stop, let the doctor quietly out, went to the corner about a hundred feet in front of me and made the left hand turn. I drove that way for two or three hundred yards until I hit a spot in the brush where I could pull the Jeep off to one side where it wouldn't be seen. I pulled in, turned the key off, and Ka-Blam went Raleigh's gun. I thought, *"Oh shit, the old fart had fallen out of the damn tree, his gun has gone off and he has killed himself."* All within about four minutes since I dropped him off.

I jumped in the Jeep, revved it up, whirled it around and tore back down there to look for his body. I go sliding around the corner and as my lights shine down on the tree, I see Raleigh hanging on with one arm, his gun pointed down toward the river. I holler, "What in the hell happened?" He said, "I just killed a hell of a big buck," and pointed into the brush next to the river.

Raleigh had gotten out of the Jeep and eased over to the tree. He very carefully started up the old rickety steps nailed there and in so doing, had reached up and pitched his rattling horns over a limb above his head. When they struck together, the ole' buck that had been lying unseen only about twenty feet away jumped up to fight whoever it was that had entered his territory. Ra-

Not Enough Bullets

leigh said the buck scared the crap out of him, damn near running over the tree.

Well, there you have it, so much for hunting at Jack Bowman's ranch where there weren't any good bucks.

As I recall, the Robinson's of Austin White Lime leased the place after that and kept it for many years. Wonder if they burned down that other house?

Bowman Ranch
Ross, MEK, Bubba Ross, Dr. Abner Ross, Bill K.

The Jack Bowman Ranch

The Vagabond Years

From 1969 until 1973 we were just like a bunch of gypsies. We wandered aimlessly over the Southwest in search of the "Holy Grail" of deer hunting. Our trek led us to the 75,000-acre Lassiter ranch in West Texas; to the Southern Ute area of southeast Colorado; to the Cimarron, Colorado area; to the Lake City, Colorado area; to the 38,000-acre Poso ranch at Chama, New Mexico; to the 10,000-acre Esquivel ranch at Tierra Amarillo, New Mexico; and to Baggs, Wyoming. Obviously, we liked to travel.

Everybody was getting a bit "long in the tooth." Born in 1899, Dad was the same age as the year, plus one half. That meant he was 68 when we abandoned the Rawls ranch for greener pastures. Dr. Abner, Raleigh's brother, was several years older than Dad. I was the youngest member of the Professional Hunters Association of America. A bunch of them were getting down to the nitty-gritty time of their lives, so we tried to make every trip count. A few we did, but most were just long, long, road trips after which we could shake the dust off of our clothes and claim we had "been there, done that."

Not Enough Bullets

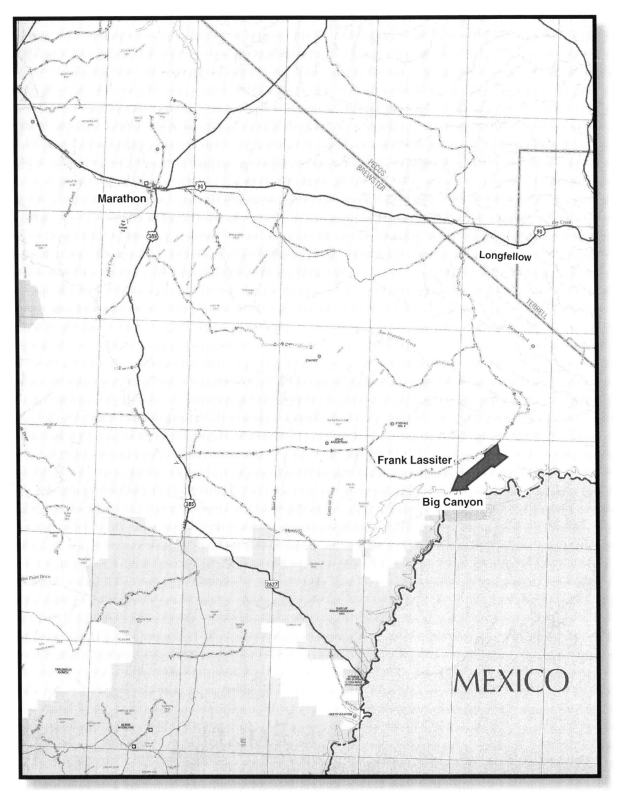

Lassiter Ranch Map Location

The Frank Lassiter Ranch

I worked West Texas a lot in my ranch real estate business and during one trip to Alpine I met Frank Lassiter of Midland. Frank was a crazy son of a gun. He had somehow managed to borrow enough money from Travelers Life Insurance Company to buy a hard-scrabble ranch down toward Reagan and Big Canyon about fifty miles southwest of Sanderson. I found out about him because some of my friends in Austin had helped him get the loan. They all had somehow persuaded Jake Beasley, agent for Travelers, to lend him more money than that sorry ole' place was worth, and he was as happy as a dead pig in the sunshine.

Frank wore, not a ten-gallon Stetson hat, but at least a forty-gallon one. The damn brim must have been fourteen inches across. The hat was so big it would have fallen down over his whole head, were it not for his big ears holding it up. He drove a beat up old four-wheel drive Dodge Power Wagon, carried a .45 six-shooter in one hand and a full quart bottle of 90-proof Wild Turkey in the other. ole' Frank was a booger!

When I visited with him that first time, I told him about us getting off the Rawls Ranch and he invited me and my bunch down to hunt on his place. He told me that one of his pastures, called Big Canyon, was cut off from the rest of the 75,000 acres and would be a perfect place for us to hunt. The

pasture covered about 30,000 acres and bordered the Rio Grande River for miles. We were excited. "Back in the Saddle Again, Out Where a Friend is a Friend."

MEK—Frank Lassiter

Enter Mr. Peace

We intended to take ten hunters with us that year, which was either 1969 or 1970. We had most everyone lined up that summer, but were still a couple of hunters short. I always attended the annual meeting of the Texas Gun Collectors Association late each summer at

Not Enough Bullets

the coliseum in Houston. One of my gun-nut buddies who usually attended the meeting was a fellow by the name of W.S. "Bill" Peace of East Bernard. Bill and I would gather up for lunch or coffee and discuss the happenings of the past year. He was into Sharps rifles and I was into 1876 Winchester rifles at the time. He had a pretty good batch of them by then and my collection of 76's wasn't too shabby.

In the course of our visit, Bill started telling me about his deer hunts down in the rice country and how he had killed a four-pointer last year and how excited he was about the whole affair. I was sitting there listened to him tell me about crawling around in the damn rice paddies shooting deer, geese and ducks when I said, "Say, do you want to go on a REAL hunt?" He looked at me and said, "Where?" I said, "On a 30,000-acre West Texas ranch in December." His response was, "When do I pack?"

On that day, at that place, Bill Peace and I embarked on a 35-year friendship that was closer than most brothers ever attain

Bill Peace — Lassiter Ranch

and was only temporarily put aside by his untimely death.

An Early Kuykendall Shot

I can't go any further without telling you a funny story about Bill. As mentioned, he was born and raised in East Bernard, a little Czech community of black land cotton and rice farmers situated on old U.S. Highway 90 between San Antonio and Houston. Bill used to say the Peaces were the only "Anglo" family there. Anyway, it was a sleepy little farming town, where everyone knew everyone. The town folk sat out on their front porches, and drank coffee and smoked whatever; and nothing happened in town that was not instantly known by all.

Turns out the high school coach was an old Aggie and Bill said he was "a mean son of a bitch." Said he'd get mad at him over something, get him in a hammer-lock, turn his Aggie ring flat side down and whap him upside the head to "learn 'em manners." After one such session of head-whacking, Bill decided to get even. "Coach So-and-so" had a big old hairy cur-dog that came by Bill's house every day about 4 p.m. and Bill decided to send the coach a message via that dog.

Bill had a single-shot .410 shotgun that handled three-inch shells. He uncrimped one and poured out all the BBs. Then, he went all around the house looking for suitable items that might work in the shell. He found a box of those little bitty black screen door tacks and thought they would do. Then while passing through the kitchen, he noticed his mother had some black-eyed peas drying on the counter top. He gathered up what he called his "personal belongings," mixed the peas and the tacks together, poured those suckers in the shell and crimped 'er down.

The Frank Lassiter Ranch

The next afternoon Bill eased out and hid in the hedge row to lie in wait for the coach's dog. Sure enough, about one minute past four o'clock, here came Mr. Cur-dog hisself, as Bill said, just a prancing along without a care in the world. Bill let him get about four-and-a-half feet past him, leaned through the hedgerow and shot him square in the ass. Said it was the damndest thing you ever saw. The old dog let out a whelp, then a howl, all the time spinning around in a tight circle trying to figure out what had just bitten him in the butt. Said the circle got wider and wider till he was damn near making the whole block, howling at every jump. Bill said, "Hell, as soon as I shot, everyone in town knew it was me and they all knew it was coach's dog too." When he got to school the next day the coach worked him over pretty good but it was well worth it.

Bill said the ole' dog lived for a good many more years but the hair never grew back over that spot, which stayed red and real gnarled looking, must have been all those "personal belongings." The story made Bill smile every time he thought about it.

Caravan to Lassiter Ranch.

Road Trip to the Lassiter

We all gathered at the Kyle ranch in late November that year to caravan to West Texas. Dad and I had our pickup with our Jeep attached; Jim Hairston rode with us. Bill drove his truck. Raleigh drove his Pontiac station wagon and pulled his Jeep. There was a pile of us. My brother-in-law Ken Koock was with us, along with Travis Eckert and Jack Maroney, all of Austin.

We got away early and drove all day going down and around San Antonio and then westward on old U.S. Highway 90 all the way to Sanderson. We gassed up everything in that little village and drove a few miles farther west, exiting the highway at what is known as the Longfellow cut-off road to Reagan Canyon. It was a dirt road about twenty or twenty-five miles west of Sanderson that ran south through the desert almost to the Rio Grande before it curled back west to end up eventually on Highway 380, the road to Marathon. This ranch road went through part of the old Slaughter ranch, Stovall ranch and by the Dove Mountain ranch. Frank's headquarters was just off that road before we got to the Stovall cutoff and before Dove Mountain, just north of Reagan Canyon. In some ways, the country is like a moonscape: hard, dry, dusty, thorny, rocky but absolutely beautiful. The natives are just the same: hard, dry, dusty, thorny, and always sucking on an ole' Lucky Strike cigarette. They knew they would die from the drought and the dust long before lung cancer even got close. Shades of Cormac McCarthy's *No Country for Old Men*.

When we pulled into Frank's place late that afternoon, it felt like we had driven 9000 miles instead of about 400. We were a tired, but excited bunch of hunters. By the time Frank gave us as drink or two, the sun

Not Enough Bullets

was going down and we still had a ways to go to get to camp. Frank lent us one of his hired hands from Mexico since he knew the way into Big Canyon, and the gypsy caravan headed out again.

"No Problema!"

As our guide led us down through the ranch on much rougher roads, he assured us all the time that everything was *bueno*.

We had asked him if we could get down to our camp in big canyon and he had answered, *"Si, Senor, hay un camino."* He didn't say, as you notice, that we could make it, he just said there was a road down into the canyon. Then I asked him if we could drive our cars down to the camp? *"Si, es posible."* Sure, it's possible to drive the cars into the canyon, but what he failed to mention was that we likely would never get them out.

Well, the ranch road got rougher and rougher and finally as we were crossing a

Big Canyon at Lassiter Ranch
The road in.

gravel draw, Raleigh got stuck as he tried to cross-pull his Jeep. We all got out of our vehicles and decided to camp there until the next day. It was about 10 p.m. by then and it had been a very long day. Getting stuck in that draw saved our bacon.

The next morning bright and early, we crawled out of whatever and wherever we had slept. We got us a fire built, made up a little boiling hot coffee, which we then poured in one of those damn tin cups you think are great, but when filled will burn the shit out of your fingers. We got in our Jeep and went up and around the little hill we were under to reconnoiter the situation.

Welcome to Big Canyon

When we went around that hill and eased over the other side the whole world fell away from us. If you have ever driven from Flagstaff, Arizona up to the Hopi Lodge at the Grand Canyon, parked in the parking lot, walked over to where the big wall is built, and peeked over the side, you know what I am talking about. There you will see just about the most awesome sight you have ever seen in your whole born days. Well, cut that about in half, and that is what we were witnessing.

It must have been a mile to the bottom, and most of it damn near straight down. They didn't call that place Big Canyon for nothing. And our little ranch road went right around to the right and dropped into about a forty-five degree slope heading for the bottom. Had we made it through that draw last night, with Raleigh in the lead in his Pontiac station wagon pulling his Jeep, we would have lost him the moment he went around that corner. I mean to tell you, he would have been gone.

We must have stood there fifteen minutes with our mouths open. Now, Frank had told us there was a tin shack down in the canyon that was big enough for all of us to sleep in, so we had not brought any tents. I took my binoculars off my neck and was in the process of scanning the bottom when I noticed a big, black spot about a mile below us and just off the edge of the river. This pasture and canyon joined the Rio Grande. Since we knew we were going to be 9,000 miles (well, a pretty long way) from any fuel for our Jeeps, we had persuaded Frank to haul a fifty-five-gallon drum of gas down in the bottom for us to use. The ranch hand he had furnished us said they had put it in the shed.

Suddenly it occurred to me that what I was seeing was where the damn shed used to be; cause it was gone! Everybody got their glasses out and commenced to help me look. All we could see of the shed was the black spot and pieces of tin scattered for about fifty feet in all directions. Sure enough, our little home away from home was gone. KAPUT!

We went back around to our temporary camp and gave everyone the good news. Well, hell, we came for an adventure and clearly that's what we were going to get. We unhooked the Jeeps, loaded everything up and around the hill we went.

The Road

I was in the lead and for some reason Dad let me drive, which was normally his deal. Well, as soon as I made the curve, we started down that road and off the face of that 500 to 750-foot cliff. I put that Jeep in low-compound and we started down. The road had been blasted out of the cliff face years and years before, and was full of loose rocks. It was so steep it didn't matter that you had the Jeep in low-low or not, you were gonna slip and slide whether you liked it or not. For some strange reason there was no guard rail on my left and the tires on the driver's side were only about six inches from the edge. Every time the Jeep would lurch and slide, my heart stopped dead. I was so boogered by it that I eased the Jeep over against the cliff wall and was scraping the right side all the way to the bottom. That's how bad it was.

Once we got down that cliff, the road smoothed out and we drove about a half-mile and came to where the shed was supposed to have been. Instead, there was blackened tin blown everywhere. Some damn cowboy from the other side had seen Frank bring that 55-gallon drum down there and had eased his horse over there from across the river. While filling his gallon jug with the gasoline he was stealing, he had accidentally pitched his Bull Durham *cigaro* into the fumes and caught the place on fire. Don't you know it was exciting there for a moment or three? I can just see that fellow spurring his horse down to the river in seven or eight, great big jumps, while that gallon-jug full to the brim with gasoline tied on his saddle is about to swing up and knock his damn head off.

Home Away from Home

We all got out and surveyed our new home. It was pretty pitiful, but being the great outdoor types that we were, we got to work to get our camp fixed up just like home. The first thing we did was build a camp fire so Dad could get our traditional camp stew going. Then we all looked though the burnt, twisted, pieces of tin to try and find the flattest ones possible. We then laid them out flat on the ground and stomped them with our feet until they became flatter still. We each chose two, one underneath our bedrolls to

Not Enough Bullets

Lassiter Ranch Camp Life
Bill Kuykendall, Bubba Ross, Raleigh Ross,
Jim Hairston, MEK, Ken Koock.

keep them off the ground so they'd stay dry, and one for the top of our bedrolls to keep the dew from getting us wet. That's what I said. One for the top, just like the little blanket your mother made for you.

We hunted out there for a week. About the third day, Raleigh and I elected to go up along the rim while others walked through the valley. We figured if we spread out and covered the whole area, something might jump up. On the way up to the top of the mesa, I slipped and fell and stuck a bunch of thorns in my butt. Boy was it uncomfortable. As soon as we topped out, Raleigh told me to take my pants down and he'd pull them out. So I dropped my pants and leaned over while the doctor adjusted his bifocals preparatory for surgery. He was sitting on a rock right behind me with his nose about six inches from my butt, when who should pop up right behind us, but Frank Lassiter. He had come down to check on us and had followed Raleigh and me up to the top. He stood there for an instant, then got that shit-eatin' grin on his face and said, "Sure hope I'm not disturbing you gentlemen!"

Raleigh and I had gone about a half mile when we looked down below us and saw that our *compadres* had kicked up a little six point buck. The deer was running out ahead of our group and they couldn't see him. Raleigh and I sat down on a ledge and figured we'd start shooting at him so the others would see where he was and help out. It must have been 600–800 yards. I got ready just before the doctor did, thought I might as well get started and tapped one down in his direction. Shot just like I always shoot, snapped it to my shoulder and let 'er fly. Hit that son of a gun right behind the right ear and he went ass-over-tea-kettle. Well, durn, I didn't mean for THAT to happen, I said. Raleigh was just getting his gun up when I shot, lowered it, thought a minute, looked over at me with a big grin on his face and said, "Game Hog!" I figured we'd get five or six shots off each just for the heck of it, but my shot had screwed all that up.

We sat there for a bit and Raleigh said, "Well, let's go clean him," and we started down. Took us about thirty minutes; that's how far it was. When we finally got down

The Frank Lassiter Ranch

to level ground and were heading over to where our group was, Raleigh, said, "Watch this!" As we got up to within shouting distance of the others, Raleigh started counting, real loud, "917, 918, 919..." until we got right up to them. "Damn," he said, "that was quite a shot I made. Don't y'all think?"

About the only fun we had was when we tried to bathe in the Rio Grande after several days of dust, dirt, and sweat. The whole bunch stripped down to our skinny, white, bony bodies and attempted to enter the water. I will tell you I think the water was coming out of a glacier nearby, cause I have never experienced water so cold. I couldn't even sit down in it much less try to splash some on me.

The only other real excitement that year was the trip down into Big Canyon and the trip out. I drove out and ground all the paint off the left side of our Jeep to match all the paint I'd already scraped off the right side on the way in.

I don't remember if we killed more than one or two deer that year. Big Canyon, while exceptionally beautiful in a rough and rugged way, had very little food and water for any game. There probably weren't more than fifteen to twenty deer in the whole valley. By the time we had run them back and forth from one end to the other we almost knew their names.

Lassiter Ranch bath day,
Forefront: Travis Eckert.

Not Enough Bullets

Lassiter Ranch Group
Front: MEK, Jim Hairston
Back: Dr. Raleigh Ross, Bubba Ross, Ken Koock, Bill Kuykendall

Lassiter Camp—Bill Kuykendall and Worker
Cooking stew.

The Frank Lassiter Ranch

Back to Big Canyon

The next year, we gathered up the old timers, added one or two new folks and made the trek to the Lassiter Ranch again. The only changes were we decided to go by U.S. Highway 290 until we got to Sheffield, where we took a back road down to Sanderson. Then the trip in was the same. That is until we abandoned our cars and changed to our Jeeps. Then, things got grim again.

The two things I remember being kinda funny in a warped sense of humor way. We went in and hunted for several days, and as the time approached for us to leave something rather peculiar was taking place. Each morning as all of us got up and hunted around for that first cup of coffee, it was interesting to note that all would wander around, look here and there and then, as if mesmerized, everyone would finally turn around and look up. We weren't interested in the hunt any more, we were more interested in whether we were going to be able to get out of that damn canyon alive or not.

We had hunted on a lot of places, but one thing never changed. We always took Dad's 1948 hunting trailer with us whereever we went. He had built it in 1948 for his first trip to Canada. It was a small, two-wheel job, built on a Model-A Ford chassis and made of marine plywood. It became such a symbol for all our hunts that we had all the names of the hunts painted on it for all to see. Each year we'd add another trip name.

Well two things happened on this trip. The first is that about Thursday, the temperature got to about 85 degrees, which is typical of deep West Texas in December. Frank Lassiter just happened to come down the mountain that day to check on us and we convinced him to haul about two-thirds of our stuff out so we wouldn't have to mess with it. We pulled the inserts out of our bedrolls, took off our suddenly worthless heavy coats plus anything else that was loose, and loaded up his pickup. He had a couple of his boys with him and they were going to unload all the stuff up where our cars were located.

About 6:30 that afternoon an unexpected Artic cold front blew in. Well, it might have been expected by somebody, but no one had

Lassiter Ranch scenery—the road out of Big Canyon.

Not Enough Bullets

Jim Hairston—Lassiter Ranch

Dr. Raleigh Ross—Lassiter Ranch

The Frank Lassiter Ranch

a radio in those days and Frank wouldn't know what an Artic cold front was if one had been published in the Midland newspaper. By dark it was so damn cold that we ran around looking for anything that would burn and pretty soon we had the bonfire of all bonfires going. We were just about out of whiskey so Raleigh hit upon the idea of pouring any liquid we had left in a five-gallon can and stir it around and, well, drink it. I think, perhaps, the addition of the bottle of Worchester sauce was probably a wee-bit too much.

The Wild Buffalo Party

By about 8 p.m., the fire was roaring, the liquid wild buffalo mix was being consumed, we all were dancing around the fire in an attempt to keep from freezing to death and fun was being had by all. I vaguely remember dancing around the outside of the fire when I got a little too close to the drop off into the river and fell off the edge. I rolled down about thirty feet trying to figure out what in the hell had just happened, when this big body came crashing down besides me. It was Bill Peace. He reached over to feel around on me to be sure I was still alive, and said, *"I just didn't want you to be alone."* Friendship at its very best!

All day Friday the camp was very quiet. We hurt so bad we were afraid if we had to move our heads or any other part of our bodies something would fall off. Not much hunting was done that day. We were leaving on Saturday, anyway.

Well, Saturday broke clear and cold and about 8:30 Frank came busting over the mountain. Instead of following the road down, he hit a horse trail about midway and threw that power wagon in compound and came sliding down the side of the canyon.

As I said, Frank Lassiter was *different!*

Oh, if I failed to tell you, the cost of the lease each year was a case of Wild Turkey whiskey. I'm not kidding, that's what it was. The only difference in the first year from the second was in the first year we had given Frank the whole case, in the second year we had kept one bottle back. You know the reason. We figured it would take a nip or two to get into the canyon and about two thirds of the bottle just to get out.

We had everything loaded on our Jeeps and Frank said he'd haul the trailer out for us. So in no time we were ready and we let Frank lead off. The lower part of the valley was smooth, so Frank took off. He ran about a half-mile as fast as he could and then made a hard right turn to start up the steep canyon road. Dad and I were about two hundred yards behind him. Two of his ranch hands were riding in the back of the pickup, which had high side panels and one was in the front with Frank. Three or four hundred yards up the steep slope, Frank started downshifting that old truck from third to second gear to get more power, then from second gear to first gear and when he reached for the first gear he missed it. As he tried to jam it, the gears started grinding, the truck stopped dead on the steep slope and started quickly rolling backwards. The little detail Frank had forgotten to tell us was the son of a bitch didn't have any brakes on that truck. I mean *NONE!*

The Wreck

Well, in about eight-and-a-half feet, you have never seen so many *muchacos* bail out of a vehicle in your life. Two flew over the top of the side panels in the back and the one in front rolled out to one side. The truck was just beginning to pick up a head of steam

Not Enough Bullets

and about fifty more yards it was going to go over a big ledge and it was gonna be "Katie bar the bedroom door." Just as Frank was opening his door to bail out, Dad's little trailer rolled over on its side and slid up under the back bumper of the truck and the whole kit and caboodle slid slowly to a stop only about eight feet from the drop-off. We thought sure as hell Frank was gonna "buy the farm" right then and there.

After the dust settled and our nerves were back to semi-normal, Frank very carefully pulled his truck up and off the trailer. The tongue on the trailer was twisted completely around, so much so, that after we unhooked it, we were able to reattach it. We opened the back door of the trailer and peeked inside. It was not busted up at all but, man, sacks of flour, eggs, guns and everything else were scattered all from hell to breakfast. Frank then towed it on out to where our vehicles were parked.

We loaded everything up, hooked the trailer up to one of the cars and said goodbye to Big Canyon and never went back. I'm here to tell you friends that case of Wild Turkey whiskey was way too much to pay for that damn place.

More of Frank Lassister

I heard tell Frank got tanked up on Wild Turkey one time over at his ranch and shot out all the window lights in his house as his guests dove for cover under the furniture. Another time he got offended by the way the names were spelled on the glass doors of his office building in Midland and blew them all out with his .45 six-shooter.

He did happen to mention to me once that he got a *"wee-bit"* distracted from time to time when that Wild Turkey started to gobble. *Really!*

Frank is dead now, probably got eaten by a mountain lion. Doesn't matter, dead is dead. Don't get offended 'cause I call Frank crazy. Hell, he was! Of course, folks in West Texas don't enunciate quite the same as you and I do. While I call Frank crazy, he referred to himself as a "crazy sum-bitch."

I liked the hell out of Frank, but he was right, he was a "crazy sum-bitch!"

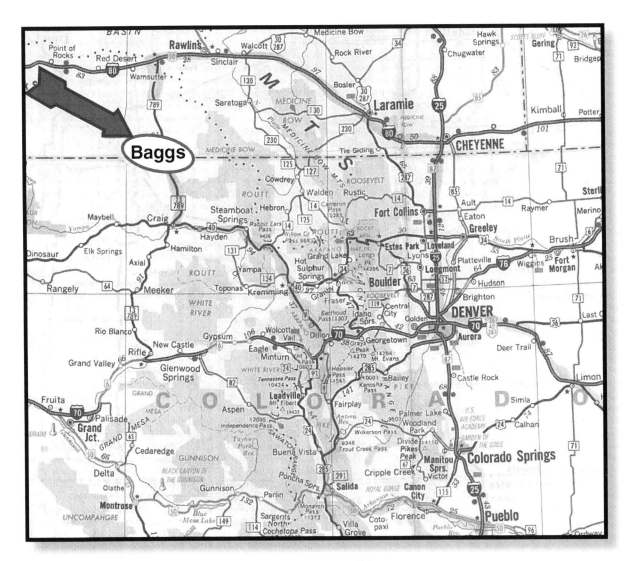

Baggs, Wyoming Map

Baggs, Wyoming

West Texas wasn't far enough to travel so we decided we'd go to Wyoming. That part of the country is a long ways by Pony Express. I don't remember who decided on Baggs, but it was probably my good friend C.N. Marsh. C.N. had hunted up that way before and I think he was the one to suggest we give it a try. The same crazy bunch made the trip, plus one or two extra.

By now, Bill Peace had his pickup equipped with an overhead camper on it, so we hooked the Jeep up to it and off we went with Jim Hairston riding with us. Raleigh Ross came and brought his brother, Dr. Abner Ross of Lockhart, along with Bubba, Dr. Abner's son. Dad rode with Dr. H. L. Williams of Austin, Raleigh's hunting buddy. C.N. had a motor home he called Big Red and attached to it, he was towing Little Red, his fancy Scout.

We all decided to go north to Fort Worth, rendezvous with C. N. at his home and take off from there to the northwest. From Amarillo, we went by way of Raton, New Mexico over into Colorado, where at about Pueblo, we angled off to the northwest on Colorado State Highway 9. Went up Highway 9 a good ways and swung a bit more northwest and headed for Steamboat Springs. We went flying through there on west to Craig, where we bought groceries and then proceeded

north into western Wyoming and the little village of Baggs. It took us two full days and nights just to get there. We looked like a caravan of lost gypsies when we checked into a fleabag motel in Baggs. We were still nearly sixty miles away from our hunting grounds. Making that drive every day was a killer.

We had mule deer permits for an area north and east of Baggs. The country was rolling and dense with a lot of sagebrush. There were some interesting high mesas with clumps of aspen here and there in the higher elevations. I suspect the country was about 4,000 feet above sea level along the highway north of town, and as you turned back east, it would rise up to around 8–9,000 feet near Medicine Bow National Forest. The names of the draws were Wild Cow Creek, Deep Gulch, Cow Creek, Dry Cow Creek, Muddy Creek, Savery Creek and such.

The season began around October 1, and usually ran from a Saturday through the next week and ended the following Sunday, eight days. I mention that because you have just passed the fall equinox. In an eight-day period in that part of the western U.S., I can guarantee that we would have an 80-degree day, a day of light rain, a day of blowing sand and dust, a day of blinding snow and then back to an 80-degree day. It was amazing.

We got situated and began to make big loops out into the high desert country. It

Not Enough Bullets

Caravan to Baggs, Wyoming

was an area of big vistas and large draws, or ravines, with the whole country stair-stepping higher and higher, the farther east off the highway one drove. We drove all day until our tongues were hanging out and saw very little game.

Interestingly, mule deer in that part of the country are very migratory. Each fall, as the weather would start to get cold, the mule deer came pouring out of that high country by the hundreds going west southwest to the Green River valley, about a hundred miles southwest of Baggs. The deer only traveled at night. In the daytime, they'd hunker down in those big, wide sagebrush draws and wouldn't come out for anything. The sage grew six feet tall in some places and as thick as the hair on a dog's back.

At night, the deer would cross the highway north of Baggs by the droves. We stopped on several occasions late at night and were just blown away by the numbers. Come daylight, you couldn't find one of the devils with a damn Geiger-counter.

Yellow Clay

That first year, it rained several times and we ran into a real interesting problem. All the lower elevations were covered with a yellow clay that stuck to anything and everybody. It balled up around the tires on all our vehicles and nothing would get it off. It would finally get so thick it would jam up into the wheel wells of our Jeeps. About half the hunt it seemed like we were down on our backs with a damn bar of some kind, digging the stuff out. When you tried to walk in it, you got taller and taller and your boots got heavier and heavier. Man, it was awful. It got where we were leaving the motel way before daylight when the ground was still frozen and waiting out in the boonies until after midnight to come out. This was just not going well.

Ole' Buddy

No need to embarrass his family by naming him, but one member of our party was allergic to alcohol. Every time he had too much to drink, which was just about any time he started drinking, he caused us problems. On this trip, when sent to Craig, Colorado to buy some supplies, he used the money to get as drunk as thirteen skunks, raised hell in some bar down there, and got his butt thrown in jail. Of course, two from our group had to go down there and bail him out, which cost us forty-eight hours of hunting time. Man, I was steamed.

We spent the rest of the hunt digging clay out of wheel wells until the week ran out and it was time to go home. I don't know who suggested it, but the decision was made to go north on Wyoming Highway 789 all the way to Interstate 80, hook a right, or east, go all the way to Cheyenne, Wyoming and then drop back into Colorado from the north. It was kinda like going back to Texas by way of Seattle. Don't know why we did it, but we did. A big bunch of bad weather had moved in on us and I think we figured if we went completely around the Rocky Mountains using that route, we might miss the worst of it.

The Long Trip Home

We took off late that afternoon and by the time we got to Rawlins, Wyoming about 9 p.m., it was snowing so hard our windshield wipers couldn't keep up. We hadn't eaten since no one knew when, so we pulled off the interstate in that godforsaken little town to try and find a café or restaurant that would be open. The good news was, we got lucky and found the only one, the bad news was, it was a Friday night. The town football game had just ended and every student and townsperson had just gotten there three-and-a half minutes before we did. Somehow, we were able to get two booths and sat down to wait. They only had about two people waiting tables, cooking and washing the dishes, all for about two hundred people. It was bedlam.

We must have waited an hour. Of course, we hadn't bathed in days, had a ten-day growth of beard, and stunk to high Heaven. That might have contributed a tiny bit to the delay.

Then, we were rescued by none other than our favorite drunk, the guy who had cost us two days of hunting. Naturally, he had already had too much to drink. As we continued to wait, getting hungrier by the second, he stood up on one of the seats, whistled real loud to get everyone's attention, and hollered: "We are from Texas and if we don't get service right now we're just gonna buy this Gawd-damn place." You could've heard a pin drop from there all the way to Cheyenne!

We Texans always try to be good ambassadors for our state.

Back to Baggs

The following year we decided we would give Baggs another try, but this time we would camp in the country and not stay in town. That would make a great deal of difference. I started lining up all the folks to go and got a call from Raleigh that neither he nor his group were going anymore; both he and his brother were beginning to get up in years. I was crushed. He had been

Not Enough Bullets

Aspen Camp—Baggs, Wyoming

Baggs, Wyoming
Telling Stories

a member of our innercircle for more than twenty years.

Minus the Rosses, we did our usual thing and caravanned to Wyoming. The main addition to our group was that C.N. Marsh and I brought our sons. We camped in a big aspen grove, put up all our tents, built a big fire, got Dad's stew in the pot and had a good hunt.

Marshall Jr.'s First Buck

One neat thing that happened on this trip was that Marshall Jr. got his first buck. He was around twelve or thirteen. I had brought along a little World War II .30 caliber carbine with civilian loads that was the perfect small gun for him to shoot. We got in C. N.'s Little Red Man two-door Scout and made a big circle through the country. It was a fine day—clear, cold, with no wind. We topped a little ridge when little Mr. Four-Pointer came crow hopping right across the road in front of us. C.N. stopped the vehicle and we both bailed out. Marshall was in the back, so I flopped my seat down and got him out. I grabbed the little carbine which I had up front with me and shucked a shell in the chamber, all the while moving Marshall out in front of the vehicle. By the time we got all this accomplished, the little buck had hopped down and across a draw to our left and was by now out about a hundred yards. I handed Marshall the gun and both C.N. and I said at the same time, "Shoot at him!"

Marshall cracked off three quick shots with that little popper. I saw the buck flinch on each shot, with the third one turning him completely around. After recovering his stride, the deer continued over the ridge out of sight. I knew Marshall had hit him, so I told them to stay where they were, so they could mark the spot, as I trotted up and

around the head of the draw. When I came back down to where the buck had been, they lined me up and I turned and started easing over the hill. I hadn't gone two hundred yards when I saw him lying dead just in front of me. I jogged back up and hollered at them that I had found the buck and for C. N. to bring the vehicle around.

When they got there, C.N and I started looking at where Marshall had shot. We found a crease under his belly, another crease across the bridge of his nose, and a hole through his side. The shot across the nose was the one that had turned him around. Then C. N. turned to him and asked, "Little Marshall, where did you aim, Son?" He said, "I aimed at him just like you told me to do, Mr. Marsh." C.N. said, "Well, you sure as hell did that, Son!" And, with that Marshall Jr. had his first buck. We were thrilled.

Some people have a natural eye for shooting. It's not something you can teach. While many folks are marvelous shots with a rifle or a shotgun, once in a while someone comes along who has that special touch and Marshall Jr. is one of them. If I may be so bold to say, he probably inherited it from me.

Marshall Jr's First Buck—Baggs, Wyoming

Not Enough Bullets

Baggs, Wyoming
Marshall Jr, C.N.'s son, C.N. Marsh, Jim Hairston, Unknown, Bill Peace, Bill Kuykendall

Perfect weather—Baggs, Wyoming
MEK, Jim Hairston, Bill Peace

Baggs, Wyoming

Marshall Jr.—Baggs, Wyoming

An Unloaded Gun

Jim Hairston and I were inseparable hunting companions and friends long before Bill Peace showed up in my life. Jim had joined us when we first started going to the Rawls ranch in the early 1950s. Interestingly, Jim didn't own a gun, at least not a hunting rifle. He lived northeast of Austin on his black land farm north of Rice's Crossing. Every year about two days before we were to leave to go anywhere, a .270 rifle would mysteriously appear at Jim's door. It would be leaning up against his back door with a box of shells on the ground beside it. Turns out Jim drank a little beer down at the store every day with all his buddies who worked there at the cotton gin. They all knew every year exactly when he was going hunting. They also knew ole' Jim didn't own a damn gun and was too cheap to buy one, so one of them who had a gun, would ease down there

every year and leave one at Jim's doorstep. This went on as long as I can remember, years and years. Finally Jim decided to build his own rifle and the wonderful neighborly act was discontinued.

We always hunted in our Jeeps with the tops down, our guns loaded for bear. We kept the magazines full and one in the barrel. You never knew when you were gonna get in a wreck and if one occurred, you wanted to be ready. The only time we unloaded was if we took the guns out in camp for some reason. Jim carried his unloaded. I bitched at him for thirty years to load that damn gun and keep it loaded. Then, damn it, you know it's ready. He wouldn't do it. Wanted to wait "til" something jumped up, then he'd load his rifle. Usually, by the time that happened the damn deer would be gone.

Every single time we got back to camp, Jim would get out of the Jeep and walk into camp holding his gun over his head. He'd point it up in the air and holler, "It's unloaded," and then pull the damn trigger. If I told him not to do that once, I told him a thousand times. "Dammit, Jim don't do that," I'd say. "One of these days that son of a bitch is gonna go off and you are gonna be sorry!" "Nah," he'd say, "Never gonna happen, it's always unloaded." Then, **CLICK!** Hell, the click alone would make you flinch.

We made a big round one day and got back to our camp in the aspens just at dark. Dad had a roaring campfire going and the stew was ready. Jim was always slow as hell getting out of the Jeep and by the time he wandered into the fire light, I'd already poured myself a drink and was sitting on one of the logs we had pulled up around the fire. About then, Jim hollered his usual "It's unloaded, see," held his .270 over his head and pulled the trigger. **KA-BOOM!** The

Not Enough Bullets

explosion of that damn gun going off under those aspens was enough to blow us off our logs. Then the thirteen remaining leaves still up in those trees came quietly floating down. We had seen some bucks that day and Jim had loaded his gun. But, as he had just demonstrated, he had forgotten to unload it.

Despite that little incident, we had a great time on that hunt. Marshall Jr. got his first buck and we killed a few others. We had a fabulous camp site, the weather cooperated and we got to drive what seemed like about nine million miles before going home. We hunted in that area three times.

Baggs, Wyoming Scenery
MEK, Marshall Jr, Bill Kuykendall

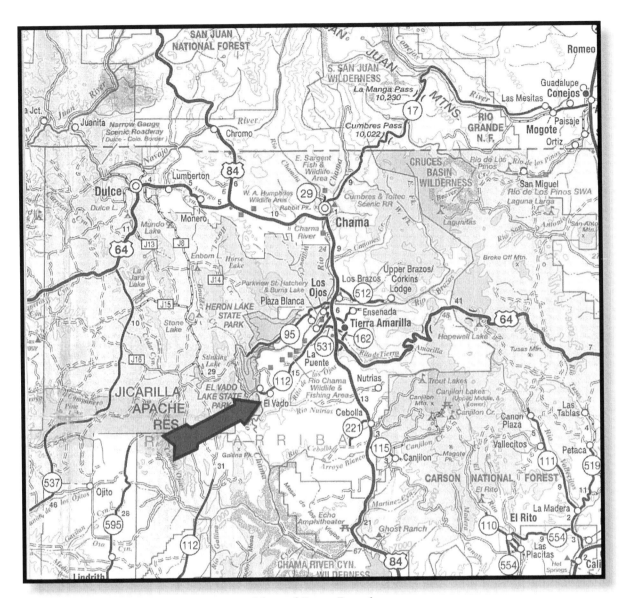

Map of Poso Ranch
New Mexico

The Poso and Theis Ranches

CHAMA, NEW MEXICO

The Austin Woods and Waters Club is a hunting and fishing club. I don't know when it was formed but many folks from the business community in Austin are members. One of the members, Jack McCreary, found out that a 30,000-acre private ranch on the west side of Vado Lake just outside of Tierra Amarillo, New Mexico could be leased. It was called the Poso. In addition to McCreary, some of the Austin folks on that first hunt were Tom McEllhenny, Jack Lyon, Charles Morrison, Walter Carrington and Ed Fleming. I'm sure there were others.

Now, in the early 1970s in Texas, if you were going to hunt a big animal, it was only going to be a deer. That's all we had. However, in the high country of the West, if folks wanted to hunt or to kill something to eat, they only killed elk. Wouldn't kill nor eat one of those damn mule deer, they said. Elk meat was their staple.

When the Texas boys showed up on the Poso Ranch that first year, they were astounded to find deer everywhere because they had never been disturbed. On top of that, there was a bunch of mule deer bucks with more than thirty-inch spreads. They said every time they drove into one of the hay meadows, there might be thirty does and fawns with several bucks. Five or six of them would be monsters. Needless

to say about the Texans who hunted this ranch, their mama's didn't raise "no boys" who were shy about killing stuff, didn't take more than a couple years to bring that mule deer population under control. Those hunters didn't want too many damn thirty-five-inch inch bucks running around, that's for sure.

Well, I had heard about all this and how big the bucks were, but the Austin boys were paying hundreds of dollars to hunt up there and you know me, if it exceeds $50 and I can't drive at least nine thousand miles, hell, I ain't gonna do it.

By the time the AWWC had the buck population corrected on that ranch, they leased another one close by called the Theis Ranch. It had about 60,000 acres and joined the Poso on the north side. Where the Theis had been game-fenced as I recall, the Poso Ranch was not. High-fencing in the west to control and manage game was unknown in those years. The Theis ranch was probably high-fenced because the owners had seen what was taking place over on the Chama Land and Cattle Company ranch near Chama. I won't wear you out about it since Texas has high-fencing everywhere now, but back then that was a rare commodity.

Anyway, I guess I have always operated under the "three ball-peen hammer theory." Translated that means it takes three good

Not Enough Bullets

MEK—Poso Ranch, New Mexico

whacks to get my attention. By the time I got up enough nerve to see if I wanted to pay some serious money, the Austin boys had moved to the second ranch. I checked in to it and I think the lease cost was $400. Damn! Now I'll pay $9,000 total trip cost to go to Baggs, have a wonderful camp, and see nothing, but durn, you mean I got to pay $400 just to get on the ranch? Well, kinda.

The Poso Ranch Hunt

By this time I had seen about a zillion big buck pictures from that region and I was hooked. So, I whistled up Bill Peace and said, "Let's go!"

Bill had his pickup-camper setup and I had the Jeep. Everyone else from Austin was stay-ing at the El Vado Lodge down at Vado Lake but Bill and I got permission from the bunch to stay on the ranch. We had a map on how to get there and it showed the ranch on the north-west side of the lake, running north for miles. We stopped in Tierra Amarillo to buy our gro-ceries and then made our way up to the very north end, about fifteen or twenty miles from the lodge. We thought we had plenty enough room to stay out of everyone's way.

It had snowed about a foot before we got there and the ground was still covered. Here and there would be a small spot where the sun had melted it enough that the ground was vis-ible. We found such a place and pulled in and unhooked the Jeep. We drug some wood in for our fire and got everything ship-shape. The sun went down and it got cold so we got the fire go-ing and settled in for our first night at the Poso.

The Poso and Theis Ranches

The morning broke clear and cold. We made coffee in the camper and then I went out and threw the tarp off of the Jeep and cranked her up to let her warm up. We drove all day. We covered every nook and cranny we could find and didn't see one damn deer. The country was slightly rolling with clumps of pinions, scattered pines and dense sagebrush. We stopped every two feet and glassed until our eyes were popping out.

We couldn't put our finger on what the problem might be until it dawned on us that it was the full moon. The moon was going to be bright the whole time we were there. Nothing will screw up a hunt better than the moon. When the moon's full, a mule deer, or any other kind for that matter, will lie up, and not move for God nor beast unless you kick them up. We made it back to camp by dark, built a big fire, had a welcome snort or two and ate our supper.

At about 2 a.m, I got up to go pee, crawled out of my bunk, slipped on my going-to-pee shoes and went outside. I walked about thirty feet from the camper and it was so damn bright from the moon, I swear, you could've read the Albuquerque *Daily Bugle*. I glanced down the flat and thought I could see something moving. I went in, grabbed my binoculars and looked. There must have been twenty-five deer down through the sagebrush feeding. I rushed back in, poked Bill to wake him up and motioned for him to get his butt outside. There were deer everywhere.

The next day, same song, different verse, we drove, we walked, and we glassed until we gave out and saw nothing. That night all the deer were back. Man, it was weird. We spent about a week up there and killed two bucks. Mine was small; Bill killed a big but thin-horned buck. Neither was good enough to write home about.

The Peace Knife

A year or so before this trip, Bill started experimenting with making hunting knives. He had been retired forever and was always looking for something to do. He got some kind of strong steel for the blades and fancy wood or bone for the handles and made two, one for himself and one for me. Mine was utilitarian, his a bit fancier. We always had them on. Well, as luck would have it, we had run into some of the Austin bunch on one of our seventy-five-mile see-nothing loops, and they told us that on Thursday night they were going to have steaks and we needed to get our butts down there and join in on the fun. It was Tuesday when we found out about it and we told them we'd be there.

On Wednesday, the weather started getting overcast and it looked like snow. It got worse as the day progressed and by the time we crawled into bed that night, it was snowing lightly. The next morning broke. It had snowed about six or eight inches and was still coming down. We drank our coffee, went out and threw the tarp off the Jeep and went hunting.

By late afternoon, it was snowing so hard, you could barely see the tow-bar on the front of our open Jeep. We realized it was about time to go to the party, took a stiff drink, crawled back in, cranked 'er back up and felt our way down the country road until we got to the El Vado Lodge.

It was pitch dark when we got there, but probably wasn't much later than 6:30 p.m. We rolled into the lodge, or better put, slipped and slid in. We stopped our trusty steed, crawled out, shook as much snow off of us as we could, and with icicles hanging from our clothes, my mustache and Bill's beard, opened the lodge door and went

Not Enough Bullets

inside. It must have been one hundred twenty degrees inside or at least it felt like it to us. The Austin guys had a big, roaring fire going in the fireplace and everyone was sitting around drinking and playing cards.

When we stepped inside we looked like Dangerous Dan McGrew and his younger brother who had just arrived from north of the North Pole. The room got real quiet and then blew up. Man, everyone wanted to come and see who the outlaws were and did we want a drink? Or twelve? We did! So, the whole bunch pushed and shoved us back to the bar and we commenced to consume just about as much as we could and maybe, just maybe, a wee-bit more than we should.

Somewhere about the eleventh drink, Bo Robinson or it might have been his cousin Spike, exclaimed, "Where is your knife, Bill? Show it to everyone." ole' Bill put his drink down, fumbled under his coat and pulled out his "Bill Peace knife." Everyone started ooing and aahing about it. About that time, the old grizzled owner of the establishment, who was behind the bar where he had his 12-gauge double-barrel hidden, said real loud, "Hell, that ain't nothing, let me show you what a real knife looks like" and whipped out his knife from some place and whacked it down on the top of the bar, as if to say, "Well, there!!"

ole' Bill didn't miss a beat. He whipped his knife out of his sheath with his right hand, picked up the owner's knife with his left, turned the blade up, and with his knife, commenced to peel the cutting edge clean off of that *son of a bitch*. I mean it rolled up just like a small piece of fine wire.

Well, that ole' man's mouth flew open and his eyes went into a squint that would have made a grizzly bear run. I thought any second he was gonna pull out that scatter gun and we were gonna be hash. Somebody at the

Bill Peace—Poso Ranch, New Mexico

bar broke the moment with a loud howl of laughter and again, without missing a beat, Bill turned his knife around and cut that the edge right back on it just like it had been. Then Bill took a paper napkin and sliced it in two to show everyone that the man's knife still had an edge on it. Right then and there the "Legend of the Bill Peace Knife" was born. More drinks were on the house, and if we ate a steak that night I don't remember it.

I vaguely remember that we actually went back to our camp some time in the very wee hours of the morning. Spike insisted we take his Buick instead of driving our open Jeep. Bill got mad and hollered at me "cause he, by God, wanted to go back to camp like he'd come," in that gawd-damn open Jeep.

I am clueless if we ever got back to Texas or not. So much for hunting on the Poso Ranch in New Mexico.

The Poso and Theis Ranches

My Father

Dad developed stomach cancer in the years between Baggs and the Poso and my hunts in the early '70s would be without him. Dr. Raleigh Ross, his dear friend, operated on him several times. The last time, he just went in, took a look and sewed him back up again. There was nothing Raleigh could do. Dad lingered until 1976, when one day short of my birthday in October, he did exactly what he said he would do. He just lay down and died. Our relationship had always been stormy, but he was the best man in the woods I ever knew; and if I was a good woodsman at all, it came from that old man.

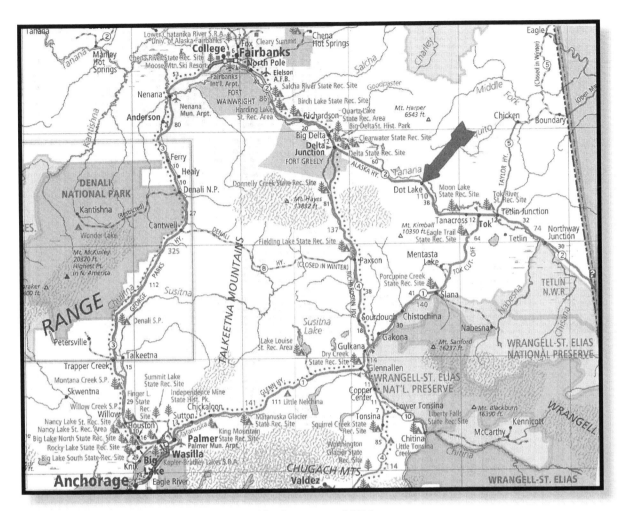

Alaska map—1974

Alaska

In the summer of 1974 Raleigh Ross called and said he was planning a big trip to Alaska and did Bill Peace and I want to go? I was on my way to East Bernard to spend the night with him anyway, so I told Raleigh I'd ask him. The hunt was planned for that fall and Raleigh needed an answer as soon as possible.

Bill and I were going to attend the Houston Gun Show, so I had pitched in a couple of my 1876 Winchester rifles in case of emergency. Sure enough Bill thought an Alaska hunt was a great idea, so we sold a couple of rifles, he some Sharps and me, the two 1876's, to fund the expedition.

The trip would be for twenty-one days, double the usual time, and was to start on September 1st. Most hunts in the west and Alaska are for eleven days. The hunters would be Raleigh, Dr. H. L. Williams of Austin, Bill and me. A few days after we all got ready and had our airline tickets, the unexpected happened and Raleigh had a mild heart attack. We needed to fill that fourth slot so I called C.N. Marsh of Fort Worth and he said he could go in place of my old friend.

For those of you who forget that Alaska is twice as big as Texas, let me refresh your memory. It is! The flight from Dallas to Seattle is several hours and the flight from Seattle to Fairbanks is just about double that. And, Fairbanks is in the middle of the state.

We all arrived in Fairbanks and were met by our outfitter, and were escorted to our hotel. Later, he picked us up and we scurried around getting all our permits bought. The hunt was supposed to be for Dall sheep, moose, black bear and grizzlies. We then went out to supper, with the "White Hunter" buying us steaks, and we paid him a big sack of money for the hunt.

Early the next morning, we got in several vehicles and headed south on the Alcan Highway four or five hours to Dot Lake, which was our jumping off spot. From there, we were going to fly into the back country to hunt in the Roberts River Glacier area. The planes used to get us back there were Cessna 180s and Super Cubs, all with balloon tires so they could land on the gravel bar of the river.

The Geese

The weather was perfect. September is a great time to be in Alaska. The colors are changing, fall is in the air, and it's cool, dry and crisp. The Dot Lake area of Alaska is the summer breeding and nesting ground for just about every goose in North America. *I mean every single one.* When we got there and started to unload our vehicles and load up on the planes, we looked out toward the west and the geese of all America were beginning to rise off their breeding grounds. I

Not Enough Bullets

won't say millions, but there were certainly tens of thousands. And the sound was wonderful. As far as one could see, here were a zillion geese rising, circling, and getting their navigational systems geared up for the thousands of miles they had to travel into the Lower Forty-Eight, as Alaskans refer to the rest of the nation.

Flying into Camp

We got our stuff loaded and over the next several hours we were ferried back into our hunting area, two at a time, and unloaded on a gravel bar in the bed of the Robertson River. The gravel bed was probably 2,000-3,000 feet across and our camp was set up on the west side of the river. The water in the

river was narrow, swift, twenty to fifty feet across and cold as hell. The water was coming out of the glacier above us and was not potable. The guides called it "dead water," whatever that meant. Our camp was located on a fresh-water stream that came from the hill behind it so we didn't need to drink the water in the river anyway.

The camp was first class. It had seven or eight tents, with two to a tent. Bill and I got one and C.N. and H. L. got one. There was a cook tent, a dining tent and tents for the guides. It was fancy.

The "White Hunter" accompanied us in to get settled, introduced us to our guides and told us glowing tales about how many Dall sheep we were going to kill. He then told us he had to go back to some other camps but

Robertson Glacier, Alaska—1974

Alaska

Robertson River Glacier
MEK—Alaska—1974

would return to the area every few days, fly the area, spot the game and drop us notes to tell us where they were. He waved goodbye, boarded his little airship and flew out with a spray of gravel. We never saw the son of a bitch again.

The area where we were located was a tremendous valley covering hundreds of square miles with the Robertson Glacier at the head of it. The terrain ran from the river area up into the mountains or either side and was covered with dense timber of every sort. There were big streams cascading down out of every single side valley. The mountains in this area of Alaska are not very high, probably ranging from 6,000 to 7,000 feet above sea level, tops.

The Wild Game

After we got unloaded, we were shown a couple of sixty-power spotting scopes that were aimed up on the slopes on the far side of the river. We all drug up a camp stool or two and were astounded to see five bull moose and three black bear feeding about a mile above us in the open areas. We were blown away. *Man, we have come to the right place*, we thought. The moose had just finished coming out of velvet and had been polishing their horns. When they rocked their heads their horns shined like a silver dollar glinting in the sunshine. The black bear were just as visible. Their coats were in prime condition. Looking through that strong scope it

Not Enough Bullets

Bill Peace and his moose.

was easy to see them as their long, black fur blew back and forth in the breeze. Their fur was so black they looked almost blue.

Hunting in Alaska is a young man's sport. There are no trails to follow and every ten feet there is some sort of water to cross. We all tried to stay dry for several days, struggling to cross a zillion little streams and the big one at the camp. About the third day, while attempting to skip across a stream using this rock and that one, I slipped and fell flat on my face in the water with my .270 underneath me. It's a damn wonder I didn't break every bone in my body. Thank goodness I did not knock the scope off. After that I just waded them like the guides did.

The countryside looked like it would be easy to walk in, but it was not. There are only a few game trails and the only ones we found had been made by the moose. They were few and far between. So, you were always walking across areas that looked deceptively smooth. The area is covered with a tundra-like stuff that is probably moss. Any way you step on it your foot and ankle is going to twist. So, we were constantly lacing and re-lacing our boots to try and protect ourselves from having a bad sprain. I was in decent shape but had decided to do some running to get in better shape for the trip. I found that was a big waste of time. As it turned out, in twenty-one days I lost eighteen pounds.

Alaska

MEK — Alaska — 1974

All you do is climb. You climb all day and then you got to climb back down. I wish I had gotten a backpack, filled it with fifty pounds of rocks and done nothing but walked up and down the seats of the nearest stadium at least two to four hours a day to get ready.

Bill and I were outfitted in the very best goose down coats and vests that Eddie Bauer made. Our Browning boots were insulated and we were ready. Well, about the third time you fall down in one of the streams your goose feathers start to soak up about half the creek and your insulated boots turn out not to be waterproof, no matter how much grease you had applied. And about that time, things started to get pretty soggy. We noted with some disparity that our guides wore wool shirts in layers and had some old single-hide lace-up Red-Wing boots. Man, where did those guys come from? Those boys would hit those streams without ever looking back, sit down for two seconds, pour all the water put of their boots, and take off again. In about an hour their feet were fairly dry and we were still sloshing around like we'd been in a damn shower stall.

The Guides

Under Alaskan law, we had a guide assigned to each of us. By the third day, I had bullshitted mine so much about wanting to "Kuykendall" a grizzly bear that he had gone back in his

119

Not Enough Bullets

tent and exchanged some pea-shooter he was carrying for a .300 Magnum. "Never can tell about these damn Texans," I heard him tell one of the others. I thought it might be fun to tap an ole' grizzly bear square in the butt with that 130-grain bronze-point bullet just to see what it would do. Those Alaskan guides did not think that was very funny.

Let me digress for just a moment and tell you a story about a young American hero. I always call anyone a hero who has been sent off to do battle in some far off place in order to protect our freedoms.

We were in camp one day resting up and drying out. We had been looking through the sixty-power scopes and had seen an individual coming off the mountain from several miles away. He was just a small dot when we first saw him then later, as he broke out into the clear areas, we could see him better. He was obviously carrying a big pack and he was moving rapidly. Later, we saw him break out

of the black timber straight across the river from our camp which must have been a mile across. He was jogging, just trotting along like he could do that all day and never break a sweat.

It took him about thirty minutes to cross the river area since it was full of streamlets and gullies including the main channel of the Robertson River. When he finally made it into camp, we found out he was a young guide from a neighboring hunting party camped on the other side of the mountain. Seems one of the hunters in that party had killed a big black bear and he had been sent to skin it out and bring it in to our camp so it could be picked up.

He entered camp and unloaded his pack and laid it up against a tree at a forty-five degree angle. Bill went over and was visiting with him and then came over to our tent and said, "You've got to come check this out." I followed Bill over to the pack which was stuffed full with a fresh black bear hide. He said, "Lift it!" I reached down to pick up the pack and had difficulty even moving it away from the tree it was so heavy much less try to lift it. It had to weigh more than a hundred pounds.

Now to the rest of the story: Turns out the young man was a Vietnam vet who had entered the war in 1968 and had his head blown damn near off in some battle. The doctors had found all the parts and had glued most of his head back together except for the big steel plate that covered part of his head. He was sent home and when he recovered he decided he wanted to be an Alaskan hunting guide. He moved up there and was having the time of his life. He had this tremendous smile on his face and he was very happy to be alive.

He was a very slight young man, probably not weighing more than a hundred thirty pounds. He had been trotting off that mountain

*Guide with MEK's Black Bear
Alaska 1974*

had seen from camp. The river bed was wide and we spent some time just trying to traverse that area without getting washed away by the swift water. Then we started up the mountain on the far side. It probably took us an hour to make our way up through the timber and out on top in the tundra and willows. No sooner had we topped out, we looked directly across from us on the other side of a deep canyon and there was a bear eating berries. That time of the year, bear hair is real shiny. The bear we were glassing would go from jet black to kinda blue depending on how the light hit him as he moved around.

There was nothing to do but go get him. So, we fell off that side of the mountain, crashing through all kinds of brush that was like Texas shinnery, until we got to the rushing stream in the bottom. We stumbled across it trying not to fall in and started up the other side. We knew we were coming back the same way so I took off my heavy Eddie Bauer coat and left it hanging on a limb. I looked around and found a little steep cut going nearly straight up, got in it and up we went. I knew if I stayed in that cut it would bring me out on top very close to the bear and that's what I wanted.

Sure enough, after about thirty to forty-five minutes of real tough climbing, pulling myself along bush to bush, I broke out from the willows, into the area of bear-berries, where I could finally see a little way ahead of me. We were climbing at almost a forty-five degree angle. As I eased up and peeked over the berries, I saw the bear directly in front of me at about 150 yards, just where I thought he would be.

Having heard that bears have poor eyesight, I decided to try to get a bit closer. But I didn't make another thirty steps before Mr. Bear stood up on his hind legs to see what was going on. I lay down, took quick

for six hours with that one hundred ten-pound pack on his back like it was a feather. Bill called to him and asked him to lift it to show us how he did it. He walked right up to that tree, tilted that pack back just a tad and then holding on to the straps, jerked it up on one knee and then swung that sucker around on his back just like it was empty. He then grinned at Bill and me and said, "It was easy."

The Black Bear

About the second day out, my guide and I took off across the Robertson River to see if we could jump one of the black bears we

Not Enough Bullets

Bill Peace—Alaska—1974

aim and shot at him. But nothing happened. My guide whispered to me that I had overshot him, 'cause he saw a white puff of smoke off a rock ledge about 100 yards up and behind him. This particular bear had a white spot right under his chin, so I reached up and cranked in another shell, pulled down on him a bit tighter and tapped him in that spot. Down he went. From the first to the second shot had been less than a 40 count.

Then the work began. We skinned him out and I'm here to tell you, a green bear hide is heavy. We cut a willow limb, tied it to it and started falling back down the way we had come, hauling and dragging our trophy as we went. It was quite a day!

The Moose

My guide and I took off one day and crossed over to the east side of the riverbed where there was a big valley. We went up that valley for several miles and then decided to top out on the left side of it. Crossing the stream that was cascading down through it, we made our way up that side for at least a mile. When we finally got out into a clear area covered with what the locals call bear berries (blackberries) we sat down so we could glass the countryside. We were high enough to be able to see back west to our camp. We also had a great view directly across the valley to the other side.

122

Alaska

I immediately saw several shiny objects and when I focused my binoculars on them I saw that they were four bull moose feeding on the far side. These bulls had recently come out of velvet and when these animals do that, they spend a lot of time polishing their antlers. For a week or so during this process, they are very easy to spot. I watched them for a few minutes as they would feed, occasionally rocking their heads back and forth, which is very typical of a big bull. I then looked at my guide and said, "Well, let's go get 'em."

That was easier said than done! They were straight across from us about a half-mile as the crow flies but to get to them we would have to completely retrace our route. That means we had to go back down the mountain, cross the stream and then climb the other side. (Remember, I said jogging won't get you in shape for this.)

We did all that, which probably took us two hours, maybe two-and-a-half. I knew where we had seen them, so I purposely angled a bit to the right. When I topped out I wanted to be about a half-mile from them.

When we got up in the open tundra where I had last seen them, we hit one of the few moose trails we encountered on the trip. Obviously this was where a bunch of them ranged and they were using this particular trail to get down to where they had a river crossing.

The Stalk

From the other side we had noticed that this area was fairly open, with scattered willows down through it and black timber off to my right. "Black timber" being my words for very dense tree growth that was so thick we always tried to stay clear of it.

The trail was very well used and was headed in the direction I wanted to go. As soon as we got out in the open only a few yards I stopped and very carefully glassed everything. I knew I was very close to one of the bulls I had seen, but there was nothing there. We went another two hundred yards and I repeated to process. Still we saw nothing. I felt that we were already in the area where we had seen the lower bull and I sure as hell didn't want to spook one before I was ready.

We did this once more and this time, way up ahead of us, I caught a glimpse of something glinting in the sun. There was nothing to brace myself against but a small willow, so I leaned against it to steady my glasses. Now I could make out a big set of horns. As the ole' bull would feed, he'd rock his head, and that was the movement I saw. He was probably three hundred yards in front of us.

I grabbed the collar of my guide and whispered that we were going to go get this one. I wanted him to watch very carefully on either side of us for the others because they had to be nearby. When I did a stalk like this I developed tunnel vision, never taking my eyes off my prey. I didn't want something to jump up from one side or the other and scare the hell out of me.

It must have taken me thirty minutes to make half that distance. By the time I had done that I could see the moose's horns but now there was no movement. The bull had lain down. His horns were level but I couldn't tell, for the life of me, if he was facing me or not. That posed this problem. If he was facing me, his ears would be cupped in my direction, which meant any little sound I made he'd be able to hear; if he was facing the other way it would be a tad easier.

When I got to about a hundred yards, I pulled my guide down and whispered in

Not Enough Bullets

his ear again that I was going to keep moving toward the bull. I told him that when the bull stood, if he thought his horns were over sixty inches wide to say the word "shoot." I was bowed up like thirteen wildcats. I was ready!

In that part of the world, you can't go twenty steps without having to cross through some water or a tangle of willows. When we reached about seventy-five yards the trail dipped down ever so slightly and damn if that sucker wasn't lying just on the other side of a little willow patch right in front of me. What to do? Well, I had to get through that patch because if I went forward ten more steps the bull was going to disappear from view. I didn't have a choice. I moved and sure enough he went out of sight. Well, shit!

The willows were wound together in a tight mesh and about twenty-five yards across. There was no wind and it was quiet. Still, those damn willows make an ever-so light sound as they drag across your $900 Eddie Bauer jacket. I knew that bull would hear me. I would take one step at a time, unwind one of the tangled limbs, step beyond it and hand that one to my guide. Then we would very slowly repeat the process.

Somehow we made it. When we eased out on the other side, we were about forty steps from that damn bull. I didn't say forty yards, I said forty steps. I was just about to make one more step when up that son of gun came. He had been facing us the whole time.

A big bull moose will stand six to seven feet at the withers (horse term for the top point

MEK—After the moose kill

124

of the shoulder-blades) and he was so tall I thought he'd never quit standing up. By the time he'd made it all the way up my guide hollered "**SHOOT**" and I shot him up high in the shoulder. His knees buckled but he got it together again, whirled and broke sharply back to my right. As he passed right by me, I tapped another one into his near side right behind the shoulders and he didn't even flinch.

He broke back through those willows as if they were nothing and man he was carrying the mail. Now, I don't think a moose knows how to gallop when they run but they sure know how to pace. I went tearing back though those damn willows as hard as I could. When I broke out the other side, he was about one hundred fifty yards away and he had it in high gear. In fifty more yards, he was gonna hit the timber. I slid to a stop, jerked up and whacked at him a third time. One second he was there and the next moment, he was gone. I mean he was out-pacing Secretariat and then, poof, he was down and out of sight. I was stunned. I knew I must have hit him but, man, no stumbling, no nothing, *just gone.*

By this time, you can imagine that the hair was standing up pretty good on the back of my neck. I tried to catch my breath and reloaded. My guide had fought his way back though the willows and we started easing ever so carefully down his way. I was so boogered by the whole experience that it took me nearly fifteen minutes to get down where I could see the top of his back in the low bushes. I eased up on him and could see he was dead. That damn snap shot had hit him squarely in the back of his head and killed him instantly. He had nose-dived into some small brush, almost hidden from view.

Many of us mighty hunters think we need our guns shot in for long distances and I was no different at the time. *Going on a major hunt in Alaska, well, better have the old gun shot in for, ah, two hundred fifty yards sounds about right.* Most all game in the United States is killed inside a hundred yards so zeroed in at two hundred fifty yards my gun was shooting about two to two-and-a-half inches high at one hundred yards. I don't have a clue how high it was at only forty steps. So when I shot high up into the moose's shoulder I actually hit the hump on his withers and completely missed his shoulder-blades. A bull moose has a hump on his shoulder just like a Brahman bull, though not quite as pronounced. It's nothing but meat. The shock of the bullet was enough to knock him to his knees but he would have survived it.

A Blown-up Tree

We rolled the bull over so I could see his right side and there was no bullet hole there. What in the hell happened to my second shot? I knew I had shot him square in that side. I left my guide to start cleaning the bull and made my way back to the scene of the battle to check it out. I retraced my steps until I was standing just about where I'd been. I eased up a step or two and low and behold, there was a small sapling about seven feet tall right in front on me and it was cleanly in half. My second shot had hit that sapling and exploded and had never reached the bull. I know my bullets and it would have been a killing shot so you can imagine how surprised I was when that shot didn't hump him up pretty good. Now I knew why.

And something to remember: The first two shots were well under a five count and I'll bet you a steak dinner down at the Hoffbrau Restaurant in Austin, the third shot was not a hair over a thirty to forty count from start to finish. I never was a slouch at getting off rounds—maybe at hitting, but never shooting.

The Outfitter

Our hunt was advertised as a Dall sheep hunt. The reason we never saw any was because our outfitter had fixed it where that was not going to happen. Alaska has hunters from everywhere but a big bunch of them come from Pennsylvania. There are two reasons, folks from there are ardent hunters and there was a direct flight into Fairbanks.

A group from that state had been hunting with our man for several years and had paid for a return hunt in this same valley. So about four days into our hunt, our head guide told us we were going to move from the main camp area to a "fly" camp about fifteen miles to the south. He told us they had seen a grizzly down there from the airplane and we might get a chance to see him ourselves. We got all our extra stuff together and made the move.

We hunted hard in that region for four or five days and saw very little. I did kill a the black bear there but not much else was seen. So after several days we told our man that we wanted to go back to the main camp. We knew there was game up there because we saw moose and stuff every time we went out. Our head guide tried to persuade us to hunt a few more days, but we insisted so we broke camp and started back to the main camp.

Strangers in Our Camp

It took us most of one day to get back. We were looking forward to some home-cooking by the cook there and getting back in our own tents. We waded the river right near the camp and walked in and to our surprise it was full of about six or eight hunters. Not only was it full of strange hunters, but the sons a bitches were sleeping in our tents in our damn bedrolls. Well, things got a little tense for a moment or two. Then those folks grabbed all their stuff and started moving out to another "fly" camp. Unknown to us that camp had already been set up about fifteen miles north, which is where the Dall sheep were located. It was an area we had purposely been kept out of so it would not be disturbed by us. Those guys had hunted the same area the year before and had good success. We had been set up and hadn't known it.

Bill, C.N and I all got a moose and a black bear. H.L. didn't pop a cap. The area was beautiful and we saw a lot of game. The hunt was way too long and by the time we approached twenty-one days we were worn out. When we got back to Texas, we filed a formal complaint against the outfitter with the Alaskan Game and Fish Commission and were able to get his outfitter license revoked.

Snippets

As I said much earlier, there are sometime-hunters and then there are real hunters. My dear friend David LaVerne Allen of Kyle, Texas was the manager of the 48,000-acre Iron Mountain ranch at Marathon, Texas for many years. He is an exceptional hunter. Every year, David would have his father, LaVerne, come out so the two of them could kill a mule deer. They would hunt for days and at some point LaVerne would see a deer he liked and he would shoot him in the ear. They would hunt for several more days until David LaVerne saw one he liked and he would shoot him in the other ear. They had a blast, loved to hunt and are marvelous shots. On top of that they saved a lot of money on the cost of bullets.

A few years ago David invited me to accompany him and his stepson out to Stillwell's Crossing in Big Bend for a mule deer hunt. We had a ton of fun. One day David jumped a really big buck. It got away from him and then came out on the side of the mountain about a half a mile away. I asked David, "Why didn't you shoot at him? Hell, just lob them in on him to see where the dust flies?" He laughed and said it never occurred to him to shoot at him that far away.

There were two fellows from Kingsland, Texas that hunted around Baggs, Wyoming every year. They had been hunting up there well before we made our first hunt in that country. One of the fellows told us that he had killed fifteen or twenty mule deer bucks with more than thirty-inch spreads from that region in the last ten years. Hell, I've never seen one in the woods that big, much less killed one. Know how he did it? He sat on a ridge for seven days without moving a muscle. He was looking through a sixty-power spotting scope over a mile-wide overflow draw.

That's where the main migration took place every year. Those deer would move by the hundreds every night and come daylight they'd bed up in that wide, sage-brush-filled draw. He would plot out the area with that scope, come across a big buck lying down, sneak down there and kill him. All the while we were roaring around in our Jeeps throwing up dust and mud everywhere thinking we were having a good time. I wouldn't have sat on that damn hill over about thirty minutes for a $1,000, nothing wrong with any of it, just different strokes for different folks.

The End of the Hunt

Hell, if you couldn't drink a little good whiskey and fall in the fire once or twice and burn a big hole in your brand new $900 Eddie Bauer goose down jacket, you just weren't having any fun. You could then hunt for the rest of the week smelling like a burnt goose. If at least one boot sole didn't fall off from sticking your freezing feet in the flames and burning off the threads, you haven't been on a good hunt. If you didn't jump some poor little four-point buck and shoot at him at least twenty-four times, the hunt was a waste of time. You then drive 900 miles to get home where your sweet wife had been holding down the home-front for a week while you were off doing *what?*

You come whistling in about 9:30 at night hollering, "Honey, I'm home," and when she meets you at the back door and you start toward her to receive your welcome home kiss she holds up the flat of her hand to stop you in your tracks noting that you smell like week-old burnt goose and dried sweat. She then points to the back washroom and holds her nose to ward off the stink. She's holding your little baby daughter on her hip. The baby's in diapers and smells like she has had the scours for a week. You hold up the plastic sack which is all that's left of the deer you "Kuykendalled" and then, with a shit-eatin' grin you say, "Look what I got."

You take off all your clothes and throw them in a pile in the wash room and she takes a smooth wire hook and pulls them all out in the backyard, throws them in the fire pit and lights it up.

After the dust has settled, being the outstanding business person that you are, you run the cost of the hunt and figure out that the deer you "Kuykendalled" probably cost you about $9 zillion a pound, but man wasn't it fun?

Life Changes

I don't want to dwell on the negative here, but Karen and I got divorced after I returned from Alaska. After that, life got very different. I was lamenting to Bill Peace about the turn of events one day and I have never forgotten what he said. But before I tell you what that was, let me say a little more about Bill. He had been stone-deaf since the Great War. As soon as he lost his hearing he figured he'd better get with the program so he learned to read lips. He could read lips in the dark, in the fog, in a snow bank, in the pickup while you or he was driving. I think, also, no, I am sure, that his other senses were greatly enhanced because of this. But one innate skill he had, something I have never seen or heard in another human being in my whole born days, was the ability to make short, concise comments in plain English. (Unlike what I have done here) They were statements that completely deciphered a complicated personal problem or anything else on your mind. You could throw something at him about how screwed up life was and he'd come right back with a quickie that in one breath cleared the issue up forever. I wish I had written more of them down, but I didn't. As for my complaints about life after the divorce, he turned to me and said, "Gulch, you jerked your stake out of the ground." And as usual, he was right.

As the years progressed, Karen became the most well known actress that Austin has ever produced. She became such a diva of the local theatre that an Austin theatre stage was named in her honor.

She wasn't as big as a gnat and when she developed lung cancer it quickly consumed her before anything could be done. About 11:32 p.m. on a Halloween night, just nineteen days shy of her 70th birthday, with our three children at her bedside, she quietly slipped into history. We were heartbroken.

Compadres

Along time ago I was allowed to join up with some older men and be a part of their hunting circle. They were men who loved to hunt; delighted in telling great stories—enjoyed campfire smoke, lovingly held their guns like babies, enjoyed shooting, savored good sipping whiskey, and while they cussed a little, they were never vulgar. They were educated, decorated war heroes and great friends. They were men's men; and women loved them accordingly. They would go down the long road with you no matter how deep the ruts got, didn't give a damn if the creek was frozen solid and always knew a horse's ass when they saw one.

So, just remember...

God Does Not Subtract
From Men's Lives
The Hours
Spent Hunting

But,

Always Carry
Enough Bullets.

Miscellaneous

MEK and ole' #17—Blue quail
Sierra Hermosa Ranch, Mexico 1958

Not Enough Bullets

MEK with deer
101 Ranch

MEK and Bill Peace
101 Ranch

Miscellaneous

Bill Peace and MEK
101 Ranch

Tierra Amarillo, New Mexico — 1974
MEK, Jack Maroney, Ken Koock, Bill Peace, Rowdy King

Not Enough Bullets

MEK, Bill Peace—Tierra Amarilla, New Mexico

Bill Peace, MEK, Unknown
Sibley Ranch, Glass Mountains—Alpine, Texas

Miscellaneous

*Marshall Jr.—Callahan
Ranch, Encinal, Texas*

*Marshall Jr.—33.5"
Cortez, Colorado*

Not Enough Bullets

Lynn Sherman, Danny Duff and Marshall Jr. in Idaho

Wylie Kuykendall

Miscellaneous

MEK — Bath Day, Lake City, Colorado

MEK in camp

139

Not Enough Bullets

Quail Hunting—Batesville, Texas
Betty Kuykendall, MEK, Margaret Kuykendall, Sarita Kuykendall,
Mary Alice Kuykendall Naiser, Marshall Jr.

Quail Hunters—Batesville, Texas
Betty Kuykendall, Margaret Kuykendall, Sarita Kuykendall,
Mary Alice Kuykendall-Naiser

Miscellaneous

MEK—Boracho Peak Ranch

Marshall Jr.—Boracho Peak Ranch

1890 Mountain Lion—Rob Roy
Bee Cave, Texas ca. 1900

Kit Carson Wallace House
Bee Cave, Texas ca. 1900

Made in the USA
Charleston, SC
15 May 2013